A Deep Steady Thunder
The Battle of Chickamauga

CIVIL WAR CAMPAIGNS AND COMMANDERS SERIES

Battle in the Wilderness: Grant Meets Lee by Grady McWhiney
Death in September: The Antietam Campaign by Perry D. Jamieson
Texans in the Confederate Cavalry by Anne J. Bailey
Sam Bell Maxey and the Confederate Indians by John C. Waugh
The Saltville Massacre by Thomas D. Mays
General James Longstreet in the West: A Monumental Failure
      by Judith Lee Hallock
The Battle of the Crater by Jeff Kinard
*Cottonclads! The Battle of Galveston and the Defense of the
Texas Coast* by Donald S. Frazier
A Deep, Steady Thunder: The Battle of Chickamauga
      by Steven E. Woodworth
The Texas Overland Expedition by Richard Lowe
Raphael Semmes and the Alabama by Spencer C. Tucker
War in the West: Pea Ridge and Prairie Grove by William L. Shea
Iron and Heavy Guns: Duel Between the Monitor and Merrimac
      by Gene A. Smith
The Emergence of Total War by Daniel E. Sutherland
John Bell Hood and the Struggle for Atlanta by David Coffey
*The Most Promising Young Man of the South: James Johnston
      Pettigrew and His Men at Gettysburg* by Clyde N. Wilson
Vicksburg: Fall of the Confederate Gibraltar by Terrence J. Winschel
This Grand Spectacle: The Battle of Chattanooga by Steven E. Woodworth
Rutherford B. Hayes: "One of the Good Colonels" by Ari Hoogenboom
Jefferson Davis's Greatest General: Albert Sidney Johnston
      by Charles P. Roland
Unconditional Surrender: The Capture of Forts Henry and Donelson
      by Spencer C. Tucker
Last Stand at Mobile by John C. Waugh
George Gordon Meade and the War in the East by Ethan S. Rafuse
Winfield Scott Hancock: Gettysburg Hero by Perry D. Jamieson
The Last Stronghold: The Campaign for Fort Fisher by Richard B. McCaslin
Sherman's March to the Sea by John F. Marszalek
Campaign for Corinth: Blood in Mississippi, by Steven Nathaniel Dossman

A Deep Steady Thunder
The Battle of Chickamauga

Steven E. Woodworth

Under the General Editorship of Grady McWhiney

McWhiney Foundation Press
McMurry University
Abilene, Texas

Cataloging-in-Publication Data

Woodworth, Steven E.
    A deep steady thunder : the Battle of Chickamauga / Steven E.
Woodworth
        p. cm. — (Civil War campaigns and commanders)
    Includes bibliographical references and index.
    ISBN-13: 978-1-886661-10-3
    ISBN-10: 1-886661-10-3 (pbk.)

    1. Chickamauga (Ga.), Battle of, 1863. I. Title. II. Series.
    E475.81.W88 1996
    973.7'35—dc20   95–51435
                                                      CIP

Printed in the United States of America

Distributed by Texas A&M University Press Consortium
www.tamu.edu/upress • 1 (800) 826-8911

ISBN 1-886661-10-3
10 9 8 7 6 5 4 3 2

Book Designed by Rosenbohm Design Group

McWhiney Foundation Press
McMurry Station, Box 637
Abilene, Texas 79697-0637
(325) 793-4682
www.mcwhiney.org

A Note on the Series

Few segments of America's past excite more interest than Civil War battles and leaders. This ongoing series of brief, lively, and authoritative books–*Civil War Campaigns and Commanders*–salutes this passion with inexpensive and accurate accounts that are readable in a sitting. Each volume, separate and complete in itself, nevertheless conveys the agony, glory, death, and wreckage that defined America's greatest tragedy.

In this series, designed for Civil War enthusiasts as well as the newly recruited, emphasis is on telling good stories. Photographs and biographical sketches enhance the narrative of each book, and maps depict events as they happened. Sound history is meshed with the dramatic in a format that is just lengthy enough to inform and yet satisfy.

Grady McWhiney
General Editor

CONTENTS

The brief biographies accompanying the photographs were written by Grady McWhiney and David Coffey.

CAMPAIGNS AND COMMANDERS SERIES

Map Key

Geography

Trees

Marsh

Fields

Strategic Elevations

Rivers

Tactical Elevations

Fords

Orchards

Political Boundaries

Human Construction

  Bridges

Railroads

 Tactical Towns

● ○ Strategic Towns

□ ■ Buildings

Church

Roads

Military

 Union Infantry

 Confederate Infantry

 Cavalry

Artillery

Headquarters

 Encampments

 Fortifications

 Permanant Works

Hasty Works

Obstructions

 Engagements

 Warships

 Gunboats

 Casemate Ironclad

 Monitor

Tactical Movements

Strategic Movements

Maps by
Donald S. Frazier, Ph.D.
Abilene, Texas

MAPS

PHOTOGRAPHS

A Deep Steady Thunder
The Battle of Chickamauga

1

TO THE BANKS OF THE CHICKAMAUGA

The Chickamauga is a quiet brown stream that meanders between steep muddy banks on its unhurried way through a long Georgia valley to the Tennessee River. In 1863 its rich bottomlands were mostly cultivated, but beyond the open fields the land rolled upward in forest-covered hills dotted here and there with a farmstead and hard-scrabble field. The farmers' hogs, cattle, and goats ranged and rooted in the woods and kept the underbrush down so that a man could see a hundred yards or more through them except in a few dense patches of blackjack oak thicket. The name Chickamauga had come from the Cherokees, and legend said it meant "River of Death" in their tongue. It had seen its share of death when white man and Cherokee had struggled for the land the century before, but it had known little but peace since then until in the third year of America's Civil War, the tides of conflict carried two great armies to its banks for one of the bloodiest clashes of the war.

Maj. Gen. William S. Rosecrans's Army of the Cumberland—Midwesterners mostly, with a large Kentucky contingent and a couple of Pennsylvania regiments—had seen hard fighting and had made a habit of winning victories regardless of initial setbacks. In 1862 they had advanced into Tennessee and fought in the desperate battle of Shiloh. That fall they had marched back north into Kentucky to blunt a Confederate invasion of that state, and thereafter they had fought and maneuvered their way southeastward through Tennessee again, from Nashville to Chattanooga. They had confidence in their commander and in themselves and expected to continue their victorious ways.

West Point

William Starke Rosecrans: born Ohio 1819; graduated from U.S. Military Academy fifth in the class of 1842; brevet 2d lieutenant of engineers 1842 and promoted to 2d lieutenant 1843, but did not participate in the war with Mexico;

promoted 1st lieutenant 1853, he resigned from the army in 1854; head of a Cincinnati kerosene refinery in 1861, he resigned to become an aide to General George B. McClellan with the rank of colonel of engineers; in May he simultaneously became colonel of the 23rd Ohio Infantry and a brigadier general U.S. Army; during McClellan's operations in western Virginia, he commanded a brigade at Rich Mountain, and after McClellan left to assume command of the Union army, Rosecrans drove Robert E. Lee's Confederates from the area and made possible the erection of the state of West Virginia; in 1862 Rosecrans commanded the left wing of John Pope's Army of the Mississippi in the advance on Corinth following the Battle of Shiloh; succeeding to command after Pope's transfer to Virginia, Rosecrans, now under General Grant's direction, fought indecisive battles at Iuka and Corinth; appointed major general of

Their brave but hapless opponents throughout all this had been the Confederate Army of Tennessee under Gen. Braxton Bragg. This was the South's hard-luck army. They were ferocious fighters who had won initial successes in every one of their major battles. Yet somehow things had always gone sour, and the Army of Tennessee had been denied the victory its valor seemed to have earned. Often the problem had been leadership. Bragg, an excellent strategist and capable tactician, was less effective as an army politician, and the fractious collection of misfits and malcontents that made up a disturbing portion of his officer corps (much against his wishes) hamstrung his efforts in command. Failure, too, could be habit-forming, as soldiers lost confidence in their commander and officers fell to backbiting and blame-shifting. It was not a happy or well-knit organization.

volunteers in 1862, he went to Kentucky to replace Don Carlos Buell as commander of the Army of the Cumberland; at year's end he repulsed Braxton Bragg's Army of Tennessee at Murfreesboro with heavy losses on both sides; honored in 1863 by Congress "for gallantry and good conduct at the Battle of Murfreesboro," Rosecrans, after a six-month lull in operations, began a brilliant maneuver known as the Tullahoma Campaign that forced the Confederates from central Tennessee into the fortified railroad center of Chattanooga and then south into Georgia; at Chickamauga, where in September Bragg attacked and drove the Federals back into Chattanooga, Rosecrans suffered a crushing defeat that virtually ended his military career; superseded by Grant in October, Rosecrans commanded the Department of Missouri in 1864; promoted to brevet major general in 1865 "for gallant and distinguished service at the Battle of Stones River," he was honorably mustered out of volunteer service in 1866, and he resigned from the Regular Army in 1867; appointed by President Johnson minister to Mexico, a post from which Grant, upon becoming president, removed him; during his remaining years Rosecrans resided on his California ranch frequently complaining of "oil seepage into his water wells"; elected to Congress in 1880, he served until 1885, rising to chairman of the Committee on Military Affairs; from 1885 to 1893 he was register of the Treasury; he also managed to have himself appointed brigadier general in the Regular Army in February and then retired in March 1889; he died in 1898; first buried in Los Angeles, his remains were reinterred in 1902 in Arlington National Cemetery.

Late summer 1863 found these two armies facing each other across thirty miles of the rugged Cumberland Plateau in southeastern Tennessee. Bragg had his headquarters at Chattanooga, a vital rail hub that was a gateway between the rich farmlands of Middle Tennessee, the strategically important and pro-Union region of East Tennessee, and the road into Georgia, with its economically and strategically vital city of Atlanta. The Army of Tennessee, grim after its many disappointments, was deployed to hold the key southeast Tennessee town. Rosecrans's task was to take it, and as week after week passed quietly after his successful campaign of maneuver that summer, the War Department became increasingly impatient for him to get on with the job.

Braxton Bragg: born North Carolina 1817; graduated U.S. Military Academy fifth in the 1837 class of fifty; appointed 2d lieutenant 3rd Artillery; promoted to 1st lieutenant in 1838 and to captain in 1846; participated in the Seminole War and won three brevet promotions for gallant conduct during the Mexican War; in 1849

married Eliza Brooks Ellis, daughter of a Louisiana sugar cane planter; after routine garrison duty on the frontier, he resigned his brevet lieutenant colonelcy in 1856 to become a Louisiana sugar planter; in 1861 appointed Confederate brigadier general and assigned to Pensacola, Florida, where he changed the volunteers he found there into drilled and disciplined soldiers; promoted to major general and assigned command of the Gulf Coast from Pensacola to Mobile; in 1862 he received orders to move his troops by rail to join General A. S. Johnston's army at Corinth, Mississippi, for the Battle of Shiloh, during which Bragg served as army chief of staff and commanded a corps; after Johnston's death, upon the recommendation of his successor, General P.G.T. Beauregard, Bragg was promoted to full general; in June he in turn replaced General Beauregard when that officer took an unauthorized sick leave; deciding to invade Kentucky, Bragg moved the bulk of his army from Tupelo, Mississippi, to Chattanooga, Tennessee, by rail, and then

Rosecrans was not to be hurried. He was determined not to move his army from its camps around Manchester, Tennessee, until he had every last cartridge, shell, cracker, and pound of salt pork that he needed to feed it for twenty-five days and fight two major battles. Only when all that was on hand, and every other possible preparation made, would he venture forward. For Lincoln this was enormously frustrating. The president had been eager to liberate the oppressed Unionist population of East Tennessee for two years now. Besides that, Lincoln had also come to realize that the way to beat the Confederacy was by keeping up a constant and unrelenting pressure. Long pauses while perfectionist generals got all of

joined General E. Kirby Smith in a bold invasion of Kentucky; checked at Perryville in October by General D.C. Buell, Bragg retreated to Murfreesboro, Tennessee, where he fought a bloody battle against General W.S. Rosecrans in late 1862 and early 1863; Rosecrans's Tullahoma Campaign in June 1863 compelled Bragg to abandon Tennessee, but after receiving General James Longstreet's Corps from Virginia in September as reinforcements for the Battle of Chickamauga, he drove the Federals back into Chattanooga and began a siege that lasted until General U.S. Grant arrived from Mississippi in November 1863 and drove the Confederates back into Georgia; relieved of command of the Army of Tennessee, Bragg became President Davis's military adviser in February 1864; he exercised considerable power and served the president and the Confederacy well during the eight months he held this position, but his appointment came too late in the war for him to have a determinative impact; in January 1865, while still serving as the president's military adviser, Bragg engaged in his most ineffective performance as a field commander: he failed to prevent the Federals from taking Fort Fisher, which protected Wilmington, North Carolina, the last Confederate port open to blockade runners; Bragg spent the last weeks of the war under the command of General J.E. Johnston attempting to check General W.T. Sherman's advance; Bragg and his wife were part of the Confederate flight from Richmond until their capture in Georgia; Bragg, who lived in relative poverty after the war, died in Galveston, Texas, in 1876, and is buried in Mobile. Never a great field commander, he had talents the Confederacy needed but seldom used: the army possessed no better disciplinarian or drillmaster; an able organizer and administrator, he excelled as an inspector, possessed a good eye for strategy, and proved himself a dedicated patriot.

their preparations just so gave the Confederates time to react and perhaps even seize the initiative.

Seizing the initiative was exactly what Confederate President Jefferson Davis hoped to do in southeastern Tennessee that summer. After reverses in Pennsylvania, Mississippi, and Middle Tennessee, Davis hoped to recoup some of the Confederacy's losses through a successful campaign by Bragg's army. He sent to find out what Bragg thought he could accomplish if moderately reinforced, but Bragg, who was in very poor health at that moment, did not believe he would be able to take the offensive successfully even with the promised additions to his force. Sadly, he responded that he would have to stay on the defensive. Davis did not believe in ordering an offensive movement by a general who did not think it could succeed, so there the matter rested.

By August 16, 1863, Rosecrans had completed his preparations and finally felt ready to move. On that day the Army of the Cumberland struck its camps and marched south again. Simultaneously, and a couple of hundred miles to the northeast, the Union Army of the Ohio, under Major General Ambrose Burnside, moved from Kentucky to threaten the other entrance to East Tennessee by marching on Knoxville. This meant additional problems for Bragg, who could not hope to meet both threats at once. Worse still, Burnside's advance threatened Bragg's direct rail link with Virginia, and if, as appeared probable to Confederates at that time, Burnside and Rosecrans made a junction and combined their forces, there might be no stopping them. As a final headache for the harassed Confederate commander, the rugged Cumberland Mountains, which at first glance might seem a wonderful defensive barrier, were in fact at least as favorable to the attacker as to the defender. They were a barrier to the reconnaissance efforts of Bragg's cavalry, and beyond them the movements of the enemy were unknown. "A mountain is like the wall of a house full of rat-holes," Bragg later explained.

"The rat lies hidden at his hole, ready to pop out when no one is watching." Rosecrans could emerge from this jumble of hills at more places than Bragg could possibly cover. With Burnside's threat on his right, Bragg deployed his army heavily to the northeast of Chattanooga, betting that Rosecrans would be looking to cooperate with Burnside.

He bet wrong. Rosecrans guessed this would be Bragg's thinking and moved one of his three corps directly toward Chattanooga to threaten the city and fake an upstream crossing northeast of the city. The other two corps swung wide to the southwest to cross the Tennessee River well below Chattanooga, some crossing by pontoon bridge, others swimming or building make-shift rafts. With the Tennessee River behind him, Rosecrans still had several impressive ranges of mountains ahead of him, and he planned now to use them for an even more daring maneuver that he hoped might trap

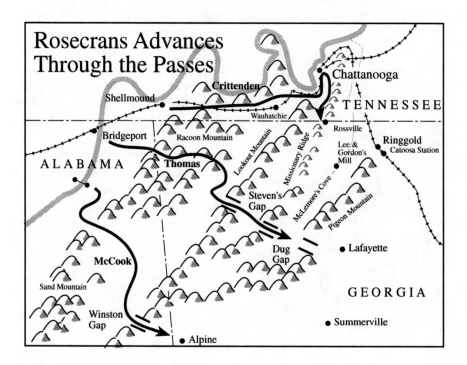

Bragg's army in Chattanooga as Grant had trapped Pemberton in Vicksburg that spring. The first of them was Sand Mountain.

After taking his troops across that broad and barren plateau and down the other side—as he set out immediately to do—Rosecrans faced another and even more formidable obstacle: the towering mass of Lookout Mountain, extending from the Tennessee River at Chattanooga southwestward all the way through northwestern Georgia and into Alabama. Its towering wooded slopes were crowned with a rocky escarpment. Taking wagons over Lookout was out of the question except at the few natural breaks in the escarpment. So rare were these gaps, that only three of them were available to Rosecrans in planning his next movement. One was the gorge of the Tennessee River itself, passing around the north end of the mountain into Chattanooga. The next was Stevens Gap, eighteen miles to the

George H. Thomas: born Virginia 1816; graduated U.S. Military Academy 1840, twelfth in his class of forty-two; assigned to artillery, he served on the frontier and in coastal defenses; he fought in the Seminole War and earned two brevets in the Mexican War; returning to West Point, he taught artillery and cavalry tactics; rising steadily through the ranks, Thomas became, in 1855, the junior major in the newly formed 2d Cavalry Regiment, an elite unit that included such future Civil War generals as A.S. Johnston, R.E. Lee, E. Kirby Smith, J.B. Hood, W.J. Hardee, Earl Van Dorn, and George Stoneman; serving on the Indian frontier and in Texas, Thomas made lieutenant colonel in April 1861 and was colonel when the 2d was redesignated the 5th Cavalry at the outbreak of the Civil War; although a Virginian, he remained loyal to the Union and was appointed brigadier general of U.S. Volunteers in August 1861; after serving briefly in the Shenandoah Valley, Thomas transferred to the Western Theater; he fought at Mill Springs, Kentucky, Shiloh, Corinth, and Perryville; promoted

southwest, and the third was Winston Gap, away off in Alabama, some forty-two miles from Chattanooga. Rosecrans could take the cautious advice of his top subordinate, Fourteenth Corps commander George H. Thomas, and take the whole army up the Tennessee toward Chattanooga, which Bragg was now bound to evacuate. Or Rosecrans could take the whole army on a long and roundabout march through one of the other gaps. Or he could choose the most daring course of all. To speed his advance and maximize his chances of catching Bragg in flank as he retreated from Chattanooga, he could divide his forces, sending one corps through each gap. The risks would be substantial, since the separate forces would be well out of supporting distance of each other, but the potential gain was spectacular: routing Bragg's army or driving it back into the trap of Chattanooga.

to major general of volunteers in April 1862, he commanded a division at Stone's River; in September 1863 he commanded a corps during the Battle of Chickamauga, where he gathered the remnants of General W.S. Rosecrans's shattered force and held his ground long enough to prevent the army's total destruction; for this he earned the sobriquet "The Rock of Chickamauga"; promoted to brigadier general in the regular army in October 1863, he was given command of the Department and Army of the Cumberland; during the struggle for Chattanooga his command, acting without orders, drove the Confederates from Missionary Ridge; Thomas's Army of the Cumberland comprised more than half of General W. T. Sherman's force during the move on Atlanta in 1864, fighting steadfastly throughout that campaign; detached to oppose General J.B. Hood's strike into Tennessee, Thomas routed Hood at Nashville in December 1864; promoted to major general in the regular army shortly thereafter, he also received the thanks of Congress for Nashville; after the war he remained on duty in Tennessee before assuming command of the Department of the Pacific; General Thomas died at his headquarters in San Francisco in 1870. Although his slow, methodical approach often frustrated his superiors, Thomas was among the very best general officers to surface, on either side, during the war. Both Sherman and Grant downplayed Thomas's contribution to their success. That notwithstanding, his record reveals the important role he played in the Federal victory.

Rosecrans chose this daring course. Ordering Thomas L. Crittenden's Twenty-first Corps to continue threatening Chattanooga directly, he sent Thomas's Fourteenth Corps marching the eighteen miles down to Stevens Gap and Alexander McCook's Twentieth Corps the additional twenty-four miles beyond to Winston. Rosecrans himself rode with

Thomas Leonidas Crittenden: born Kentucky 1819, the son of U.S. Senator John J. Crittenden, younger brother of Confederate General George B. Crittenden, and first cousin of Union General Thomas T. Crittenden; admitted to the bar in 1840 and in 1842 elected commonwealth attorney for his district; participated in the war with Mexico, serving successively as aide to General Zachary Taylor and as colonel of the 3rd Kentucky Infantry, whose major was John Cabell Breckinridge, later Vice-President of the U.S. as well as a Confederate major general and Secretary of War; in 1849 President Taylor appointed Crittenden consul at Liverpool; in 1853 he returned

to Kentucky, residing in Frankfort and Louisville; adhering to the Union, as did his father, Crittenden became commander of state forces that remained loyal after General Simon B. Buckner led the others south for service in the Confederacy; commissioned a brigadier general of volunteers in September 1861; the following spring, Crittenden commanded the Fifth Division of Don Carlos Buell's Army of the Ohio, which arrived in time to reinforce U.S. Grant's forces at the Battle of Shiloh; during the campaigns of Tullahoma and Chickamauga, Crittenden served as one of General William S. Rosecrans' principal lieutenants, commanding the Twenty-first Corps in the latter campaign; subsequently, Rosecrans attempted to transfer some of the responsibility for the disaster at Chickamauga by preferring charges against Crittenden, as well as against Generals Alexander McD. McCook and James S. Negley; all were formally acquitted following an exhaustive inquiry conducted at Nashville, but none of their military careers flourished thereafter; Crittenden resigned his volunteer commission in December 1864 and in January 1866 was appointed state treasurer of Kentucky; subsequently, President Andrew Johnson offered him a colonelcy in the Regular Army, which Crittenden accepted, serving until retirement in 1881; he died on Staten Island, New York, in 1893, and was buried in Frankfort, Kentucky.

Thomas in the middle column, and on September 8 he learned that his plan was beginning to have its effect. A dispatch from Crittenden announced that Bragg had abruptly abandoned

Alexander McDowell McCook: born Ohio 1831, the highest ranking of the fourteen "Fighting McCooks" who participated in the Civil War; he was the brother of Daniel McCook, Jr., and of Robert Latimer McCook; Edward Moody McCook was his first cousin; he graduated from the U.S. Military Academy in 1852, requiring five years to complete the four-year course, and was posted to the 3rd Infantry; served on the frontier and then as instructor of tactics at West Point until the outbreak of the Civil War; four days after the surrender of Fort Sumter, he was commissioned colonel of the 1st Ohio Volunteers, which he led at First Bull Run in July; appointed brigadier general of volunteers in September 1861, he commanded a brigade in Kentucky and the Second Division of the Army of the Ohio, under Don Carlos Buell, at the capture of Nashville, the Battle of Shiloh, and the subsequent "siege" of Corinth; he was promoted to major general in July 1862;

McCook commanded the Twentieth Corps during the battles and campaigns of Perryville, Murfreesboro, Tullahoma, and Chickamauga; in the latter he was blamed, along with T.L. Crittenden, for the Union disaster; although subsequently officially exonerated by a court of inquiry, which he had himself requested, he was not again given command of troops in the field and awaited orders until November 1864; nevertheless, McCook was awarded the brevets of brigadier and major general in the Regular Army at the war's end, but McCook's rank of captain, 3rd Infantry, was not augmented, certainly a unique circumstance for one who was a major general of volunteers and by brevet in the Regulars; nevertheless, he remained in the army, discharging much duty on the frontier and as aide to General W.T. Sherman; moreover, through the years McCook managed to advance in rank, to lieutenant colonel, 26th Infantry, in 1867, to colonel in 1880, to brigadier general in 1890, and to major general in 1894; he retired in 1895, and in 1896 represented the United States at the coronation of Nicholas II of Russia; he died in Dayton, Ohio, in 1903, and was buried in Cincinnati.

Chattanooga and was fleeing toward Atlanta. In the days that followed, the delighted Rosecrans believed he saw further confirmation of his success as a steady stream of Confederate deserters straggled into Union lines all giving the same story: the Army of Tennessee was demoralized and at the point of falling to pieces. Eagerly Rosecrans pushed his excited soldiers forward in hopes of finishing the job.

Rosecrans's belief about the Army of Tennessee was a very dangerous one, for it was precisely what Bragg wanted him to think. In fact, the Army of Tennessee, though discouraged at its losses in territory, was still full of fight, and Bragg was looking for one. Most of those ostensible deserters had in fact been primed by Bragg to create just the right impression on Rosecrans, and the trick was working. In recent weeks the situation of the Army of Tennessee had excited increasing concern in Richmond, and the authorities there had decided to do something about it. Reinforcements were soon on their way to Bragg from Mississippi and Virginia, and Major General Simon B. Buckner's Corps from East Tennessee, unable to stop Burnside's steady advance, came down to join Bragg. The Virginia contingent, two divisions under Lieutenant General James Longstreet, would take some ten days in transit since due to the loss of East Tennessee, they would have to ride the rails on a roundabout route down the Eastern seaboard and then back up through Atlanta. Even without them, however, Bragg had by this time some 55,000 men, a good 15,000 more than he had been able to muster only a few weeks before, and just 7,000 fewer than Rosecrans had.

He concentrated his newly powerful army in a position to block Rosecrans from advancing against the Confederate supply line once he cleared the mountains. His line faced west, with his left at La Fayette, Georgia, and his right at Lee and Gordon's Mill, where the road from La Fayette to Chattanooga crossed Chickamauga Creek. That put him directly in front of the center column of Rosecrans's far-flung army. Bragg ordered his cavalry to delay the advance of the outside Federal columns and prepared to give Rosecrans a warm reception as soon as he stuck the head of his column out of those hills.

He did so on September 9. That afternoon Thomas's lead division, that of Major General James S. Negley, swung down off Lookout and camped along the upper reaches of Chickamauga Creek, little more than half a dozen miles west of La Fayette and separated from that town by a spur of Lookout Mountain called Pigeon Mountain. Pigeon angled off northeastward from the main ridge of Lookout about a dozen miles to the south. Inside the angle formed by Pigeon and Lookout were the headwaters of Chickamauga Creek, in a pleasant and fertile cul-de-sac of a valley known as McLemore's Cove. If Bragg had his way, the cove would not be at all pleasant for Thomas, for he intended to shove as much of the Union general's corps as possible back into it with no option but surrender or dispersal.

Bragg knew he had no time to lose. The opportunity before him was such as came to a general once in two lifetimes, and it would not last long once the Union flanking columns began to close in. Bragg gave immediate orders for Lieutenant General D.H. Hill, commanding one of his corps at La Fayette, to push the crack division of Major General Patrick R. Cleburne over Pigeon Mountain by way of Dug Gap to fall on the unsuspecting Federals. At the same time Bragg sent orders for Major General Thomas C. Hindman to sweep south from his position at Lee and Gordon's Mill, up the Chickamauga to complete Negley's destruction—along with the destruction of whatever additional troops Thomas might be cooperative enough to send down the west slope of Lookout and into the maw of this two-headed Confederate monster. In case all that was not enough, the rest of the Army of Tennessee was closed up and ready to move behind Hindman's and Cleburne's lead divisions in full support.

Hindman started well. He made the night approach march

as ordered by Bragg and got into position to make his flank attack. Then his nerve deserted him. He halted and began to contemplate unknown dangers lurking beyond Lookout and conjured up by his imagination. Bragg urged him on, but to no avail. In what amounted to disobedience to orders, he stayed where he was. Hill proved even worse, for he made no start at all. Instead, he sent Bragg a stream of complaints, excuses, and ill-founded fears. On him, too, reiterated orders had no effect. Hill had been purged from Robert E. Lee's army because, despite occasional good performances, he had displayed shocking lapses as well as a carping and insubordinate spirit. Bragg was just beginning to learn about this for himself. By the time Bragg finally got his balky army into motion the next afternoon, September 11, Negley had learned of his danger and pulled back onto Lookout Mountain. The opportunity was lost.

Then, incredibly, another and even better opportunity beckoned. Crittenden, with his Twenty-first Corps, having occupied Chattanooga September 9, the day after Bragg pulled out, had been pushing south along the Chattanooga and La Fayette Road (generally called simply the La Fayette Road). As Bragg had waited in vain for Hill and Hindman to obey orders and crush Negley, Crittenden's men had been gradually driving back the outposts on his right flank, finally forcing him to abandon Lee and Gordon's Mills and pull back to the east bank of the Chickamauga. That had seemed bad at the time, but now with Negley recoiling to the west after his brush with disaster and McCook still well to the south, Crittenden was extremely vulnerable. Once again Bragg reacted alertly. At 3 A.M., September 12, he ordered Lieutenant General Leonidas Polk to take his own corps and that of Major General William H.T. Walker, thirteen brigades in all, and hit Crittenden's nine brigades in front and flank. Polk started out, got into position, and then balked, complaining he had not enough men. Bragg ordered up Buckner's Corps as well, another seven brigades, giving Polk, the senior officer present, a two-to-one numerical superiority, but still Polk would not move. A pompous and ingratiating man, appointed major general directly from civilian life (he was an Episcopal bishop) early in the war by his old West Point friend Jefferson Davis, Polk had by now established a long habit of disobeying Bragg's orders. And so, to Bragg's unspeakable frustration, this opportunity too was allowed to slip away. Opportunity such as many generals would never get at all had come to Bragg not once but twice in a single week. The Army of the Cumberland had been in his power, his to destroy, easily, cheaply, piece-by-piece, and he could not get his generals to carry out the orders that would have made it happen.

By this time, Rosecrans's delusion was beginning to wear off. Indications at his headquarters were that the Rebel force that Negley had brushed against in McLemore's Cove September 11 had been no mere rear-guard but major elements of the Army of Tennessee. Additional intelligence seemed to indicate that Bragg was now full of fight and fully concentrated somewhere near La Fayette and, even worse, that substantial reinforcements were on their way to Bragg from Virginia and might even now be in his ranks. Rosecrans reacted correctly, ordering both of his flanking columns, McCook and Crittenden, to close in on the center and unite with Thomas to concentrate the army and prepare to defend against a probable attack. Still, the discovery had been a shock, and Rosecrans seemed somehow not quite right. A high-strung, nervous man at the best of times, he was keyed up to fever pitch for this campaign and had not been taking proper food or rest for some days. The strain now began to show, both in his demeanor and in a slight and as yet insignificant tendency to give confusing orders.

After the depressing failures of his two attempts to defeat Rosecrans in detail, Bragg apparently decided to wait until his Virginia reinforcements came up. By the evening of September

17, Rosecrans, headquartered in the stately Gordon-Lee
Mansion half a mile west of Lee and Gordon's Mill, finally had
his three corps within supporting distance of each other and
could breathe somewhat easier. His line faced east, toward
Chickamauga Creek, with his left (or northern) flank at Lee
and Gordon's Mill. The next morning, the Army of Northern
Virginia troops began arriving in Bragg's lines, boosting his
numbers to about 65,000 against Rosecrans' 62,000. The
Confederate general prepared to make his move. His plan was
to turn Rosecrans's left, getting between the Federals and
Chattanooga, and then push them southward to their destruction in McLemore's Cove, doing to the whole Army of the
Cumberland what he had anticipated doing to Negley's division
nine days before.

The first step was to seize the crossings of Chickamauga
Creek, in order to put the army on the west side and in position to sweep down on Rosecrans's flank at Lee and Gordon's,
but Rosecrans had alertly covered these crossings with cavalry, and by mid-morning, September 18, fighting flared up near
two key bridges. At Alexander's Bridge, about three miles
northeast of Lee and Gordon's Mill, the Federal covering force
was the "Lightning Brigade," four regiments of mounted
infantry under the command of Colonel John T. Wilder, an
Indiana businessman turned uncommonly good soldier.
Wilder's men were tough, confident veterans from Illinois and
Indiana who prided themselves on being not cavalry but
infantry, and therefore serious fighters. Hunkered down behind
makeshift breastworks on the stream's west bank, they now
turned in a very serious piece of fighting indeed, as a whole
division of Confederates set out to storm the crossing. The
Southerners belonged to Liddell's Division of Walker's Corps,
and they were driven back again and again by the torrent of
firing from the far bank. What they were encountering was not
just one of the better brigades in the Army of the Cumberland
but also the unusual new weapons with which it was equipped.

Wilder's men were carrying not the typical single-shot, muzzle-loading rifle of the Civil War, but seven-shot Spencer repeating rifles. These powerful weapons could fire six or seven times as fast as the standard issue Civil War weapon, and Wilder's men were giving notice that they knew how to use them. The Confederate attack at Alexander's Bridge went nowhere.

Another mile and a half further north lay Reed's Bridge. It was covered by a brigade of Union cavalry under Brigadier General Robert H.G. Minty. Their job was more difficult. The meanderings of the creek at this point made the west bank an untenable position and a potential trap for defenders. If Reed's

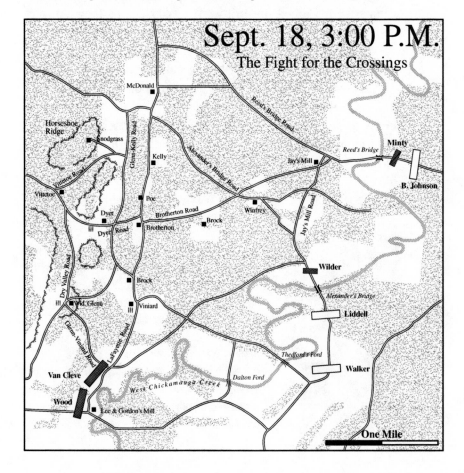

Sept. 18, 3:00 P.M.
The Fight for the Crossings

Bridge was to be held, it would have to be done about a quarter mile to the east, at Pea Vine Ridge, where the road came through a notch on its way to the creek. Minty was a good officer and tried. For most of the day, he enjoyed success, as a frustrated Confederate Brigadier General Bushrod R. Johnson endeavored to push his division forward without needed cavalry to let him know what was ahead. Late that afternoon, after repeated attempts to force a column through the notch, Johnson shook out a brigade in line of battle and sent them scrambling up and over the ridge. That was too much for Minty and his cavalry, who saddled up and rode. The blue-jacketed troopers tried to set fire to the rickety bridge as they left, but Johnson's hard-charging Confederates were on them too fast.

With Reed's Bridge in their hands, Southerners swarmed across and quickly flanked Wilder out of his position behind Alexander's Bridge. More Confederates poured onto the west bank, as darkness brought an end to the final skirmishes between the victoriously advancing Confederates and the retiring Union covering forces. By morning, Bragg had the bulk of his army across Chickamauga Creek and ready to implement his plan.

For Rosecrans it had been a tense day of partial and confusing intelligence reports, and it had

John Thomas Wilder: born New York 1830; became lieutenant colonel of the 17th Indiana Volunteer Infantry in 1861; promoted to colonel in 1862; at his insistence the regiment was mounted and armed with Spencer repeating rifles; commanded Wilder's Mounted Brigade, and later a cavalry corps in the Army of the Cumberland; brevetted brigadier general in 1864 for "war service"; resigned his commission in October 1864. After the war he became an industrialist and developer of Tennessee's railroads and coal fields. He died in 1917.

ended without giving him any clear idea of just what Bragg's army was up to or where it was. Still, sensing that the Confederate commander must be clawing at the Federal left flank, Rosecrans decided on the first of a series of convoluted maneuvers that would serve him well only as long as his over-heated yet fatigue-dulled mind could keep up with their steadily increasing degree of complication. He ordered Crittenden, on the Federal left, to shuffle his two right divisions around to the left. Then he directed three of the four divisions of Thomas's Corps to pull out of the center of the Union line, pass

Bushrod R. Johnson: born Ohio 1817; graduated from the U.S. Military Academy in 1840, twenty-third in his class of forty-two that included W.T. Sherman, G.H. Thomas, and R.S. Ewell; commissioned 2d lieutenant and posted to the 3d Infantry, he served on the frontier, in the Seminole War, and in Mexico; promoted to 1st lieutenant in February 1844; he resigned his commission in 1847 to become an educator; an instructor and administrator at the Western Military Institute in Kentucky and the Military College of the University of Nashville, Johnson was also active in both the Kentucky and Tennessee militias; he entered Confederate service as a colonel of engineers in June 1861 and was appointed brigadier general the following January; forced to surrender with the garrison at Fort Donelson in February 1862, he managed to escape through Union lines; wounded while leading a brigade at Shiloh, he recovered to lead his brigade in General Braxton Bragg's invasion of Kentucky and at Murfreesboro; commanded a provisional division at Chickamauga and directed General Simon B. Buckner's Division at Knoxville; transferred to the Eastern Theater, he led a brigade in the early defense of Petersburg; promoted to major general, he commanded a division in the Petersburg trenches and took part in restoring the Confederate line during the Battle of the Crater in July 1864; relieved of duty after his division was destroyed at Sayler's Creek in April 1865, he was without a command when he surrendered at Appomattox; after the war he became chancellor of the University of Nashville. General Johnson died at his farm near Brighton, Illinois, in 1880.

entirely behind Crittenden, and march all night up the Dry Valley Road before crossing to the La Fayette Road near the modest house and outbuildings of a farmer named Kelly, in order to be in position to block any attempt by Bragg to get between the Army of the Cumberland and Chattanooga.

First light was just spreading across the woods and scattered fields west of Chickamauga Creek the next morning, September 19, as the first of Thomas's divisions, that of Brigadier General John M. Brannan, reached the Kelly Field and, on orders, fell out of ranks, dropped to the ground and either went to sleep or, inevitably for Civil War soldiers, set about boiling coffee. They were to have neither sleep nor breakfast, however. Just minutes later, orders came to form ranks again. Reports indicated a single Confederate brigade might be between their position and Chickamauga Creek, easy picking for an alert attack. Thomas wanted those Confederates snapped up. Resignedly, the bluecoats heaved themselves to their feet and formed up, shouldering their rifles and hitching their cartridge boxes around to hang more conveniently. Then the lead brigade plunged forward into the woods.

2
ENCOUNTER IN THE WOODS

Thomas's idea that a lone Confederate brigade was west of Chickamauga Creek was, of course, a serious misconception. Practically the whole Rebel army was there. But Thomas was far from the only one to suffer from misconceptions on what was to become one of the most confused days of battle for either army during the whole war, as Rosecrans shuffled and re-shuffled his army northward up the La Fayette Road even as it fought, and Bragg probed and lunged at the Army of the Cumberland in the effort somehow to draw a bead on this bewildering array of targets that seemed to shift constantly in these opaque woodlands and could also strike back with painful effectiveness.

Bragg's misconception that morning was that the Federal left still rested on Lee and Gordon's Mill. Since he had his army on the west bank of Chickamauga Creek well north of the mill, he assumed that he had succeeded in his goal of turning

Rosecrans and now needed only to drive down on the Federal flank and hurl the bluecoats to their destruction in McLemore's Cove. It was as Bragg was preparing to launch this advance that Thomas's advance struck what was supposed to be his right rear. Covering that flank was the cavalry of Major General Nathan Bedford Forrest, a former slave-trader

Nathan Bedford Forrest: born Tennessee 1821; received little formal education, but by the outbreak of the Civil War he had acquired a substantial fortune as a planter and slave dealer; enlisted as a private in the 7th Tennessee Cavalry, raising and outfitting at his own expense a battalion of mounted troops that elected him lieutenant colonel in October 1861; during the seige of Fort Donelson, he asked and received permission for his men to break through Union lines and escape surrender; elected colonel of the 3rd Tennessee Cavalry just before Shiloh; in June 1862 assumed command of a cavalry brigade, and the following month captured a Union garrison

and its stores at Murfreesboro; promoted to brigadier general, he severed Grant's communications in West Tennessee in December, and in May 1863 saved the railroad between Chattanooga and Atlanta; he participated in the Chattanooga Campaign, but a quarrel with General Bragg caused him to ask for and receive from President Davis an independent command in North Mississippi and West Tennessee; when promoted to major general in December 1863 his fame as a cavalryman had become legendary and "his exploits went unabated till the end of the war"; he captured Fort Pillow in April 1864; in June he brilliantly routed a superior force at Brice's Cross Roads; and the following month he checked General A.J. Smith at Tupelo; such lightning blows alarmed General Sherman; Forrest commanded all cavalry under John Bell Hood in the Tennessee Campaign; promoted to lieutenant general in February 1865, Forrest was finally overwhelmed by superior forces at Selma, Alabama, in April 1865. After the war, he returned to planting and was for some years president of the Selma, Marion & Memphis Railroad, which he helped promote. He died, probably of diabetes, at Memphis in 1877, and is buried there. Several military authorities believe he was the greatest cavalry officer produced in America.

turned thoroughly unorthodox but very hard-fighting cavalry leader. The first warning many of Forrest's men got was the sound of thousands of boots crunching over the dry leaves in the stillness of the frosty morning. Suddenly out of the woods about a hundred yards away emerged a full Union battle line. One of Forrest's troopers recalled that they had been "resting, rearranging saddles and girths, and incidentally munching hardtack...all resting easy that there was not a Yankee within cannon range," when they were startled by the crash of musketry aimed at their pickets. "By thunder," gasped a startled Confederate, "That's infantry." Recovering from the initial

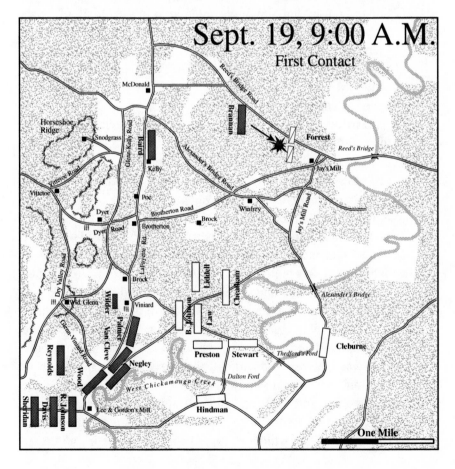

shock Forrest's men settled down to a stubborn dismounted fight, their commander grimly holding them to the work. Forrest's two brigades of cavalry were soon supported by infantry from Walker's corps, and a full-scale battle raged.

If the Confederates were surprised, their opponents were only slightly less so. Commanding Brannan's lead brigade was twenty-six-year-old Yale graduate Colonel John Croxton, whom Thomas considered the best soldier to come out of Kentucky during the whole war—a bold word indeed. This fighting, however, was unlike any the young Kentuckian had yet encountered. The woods were open enough to form and maneuver lines of battle, but visibility was limited to the length of a single regiment's line. It was hard to say what Rebels were out there, only that there seemed to be a great many and all firing very fast. Wryly Croxton sent back to Thomas to find out which of the five or six brigades in his front was the one he was supposed to capture.

Croxton soon had little enough to laugh about. His cavalrymen all but exhausted, Forrest threw forward the two brigades of infantry he had received as reinforcements. On the Federal left, the attack went nowhere, running head on into the brigade of Colonel Ferdinand Van Derveer, one of the hardest fighting units in the Army of the Cumberland. Van Derveer's men easily repulsed the Confederate infantry, then about-faced and swung their line backward like a gate on its hinges to demolish an attempted flanking attack by one of Forrest's cavalry brigades that had caught its breath and come back into the battle. Van Derveer's men put it out of the fight for good.

On the Union right, however, it was a different story. There the Confederate line loomed up out of the underbrush a hundred yards away and almost squarely athwart the flank of Croxton's brigade, and there was not a thing in the world the young Yale man could do about it since the woods hid each side from the other until contact was first made within easy rifle range. Then whichever side happened to be in the better position won. Accordingly, Croxton's regiments got roughed up and thrown back westward toward the La Fayette Road.

Thomas, hearing the rising volume of firing in the woods east of Kelly Field, had taken action to tip the scales in favor of the Union. The division of Brigadier General Absalom Baird was already tramping through the woods to come up on Brannan's right. When Baird hit, the combat situation was suddenly reversed. The Confederate line, facing northwest, had struck Brannan's right flank. Now Baird, with his line facing northeast, struck the Confederate left and sent the Southerners scattering back in disorder toward the Chick-

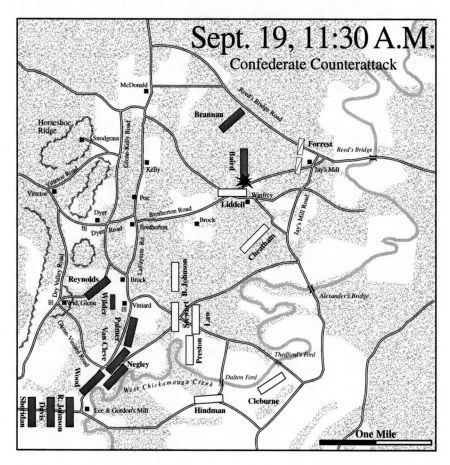

amauga. For a few minutes Baird's men exulted over their success, only to suffer their own dramatic reversal. Walker's other division, that of Brigadier General St. John R. Liddell, was sent into the rapidly growing battle and crashed into Baird's flank, breaking his three brigades one after the other and routing his division. By now Brannan's division had regained its equilibrium and counterattacked to restore the situation. Conspicuous once again was Van Derveer's brigade, particularly its 9th Ohio, an all-German unit recruited in Cincinnati and given to impetuous bayonet charges. Another of their mad rushes helped hurl back Liddell's troops and recapture the derelict guns of an abandoned Union battery.

It was now about midday, and the Federals had not done badly at all. Walker's Corps had been savaged and driven back several hundred yards from its morning position. The situation was quite contrary to what Bragg had expected to find, and it took him some time to figure it out and decide what to do next. The most immediate need, it turned out, was to give some kind of help to Walker. So, shortly after noon, Bragg sent in the division of Major General B. Franklin Cheatham. An oversized formation with five brigades, Cheatham's Division was larger than Walker's whole corps. It might have swung the tide of battle dramatically if not for the fact that at about the same time Rosecrans sent in two more divisions of his own, just arriving after marching up from Lee and Gordon's Mill.

In keeping with the Union commander's ever more complex manner of directing this battle, the two fresh divisions represented two different corps of his army, neither of them Thomas's, which, thanks to a traffic jam the night before, still had only two of its own divisions on hand. Johnson's division belonged to the Twentieth Corps, Palmer's to the Twenty-first. Side by side they moved eastward from the La Fayette Road, overlapping the area of previous fighting and extending the battle lines farther south. At the same moment, Cheatham's brigades were moving in the opposite direction, and as the two lines crashed into each other at close rifle range, the roar of battle rose to a new crescendo.

Johnson's division, on the left, met with spectacular success. Sparked by the hard-driving performance of the brigade of Brigadier General August Willich, a Prussian-trained immigrant who had started the war as a private in the 9th Ohio, the division flattened Cheatham's right-flank brigade and surged eastward across fought-over ground that Cheatham's men had only just recovered.

Palmer, on the right, faced the bulk of Cheatham's force but was spared the fate of other Federal units before him when encountering Confederates advancing unexpectedly through the woods. As Palmer had been forming up along the La Fayette Road preparatory to his advance, Rosecrans had sent a note suggesting the division move out in echelon, that is, left brigade leading, center brigade a few hundred yards to the right and rear, right brigade still further to the right and rear. Clearly the Federal commander had grasped—on the basis of little more than the sound of the firing and such fragmentary reports as he could get—what had happened to Baird's division. If Confederate troops were advancing diagonally across his front through the woods and tending to strike his units on their right flanks, he would remedy that by preparing the units to turn and fight in that direction. The advice proved just right, for Cheatham was advancing to the south of but along roughly the same axis as Walker's divisions. Palmer's echeloned line met him squarely and stopped him.

On the left of the Federal division, next to Johnson's position, the brigade of William B. Hazen struck the Confederates in a broad cornfield belonging to a farmer named Brock, and a vicious close-range firefight developed. Hazen's men emptied their cartridge boxes, were briefly relieved by other troops that had hastened up from the south, drew another forty rounds per man from the ordnance wagons, and returned to the fight in the Brock Field. Before the afternoon was over, they had repeated the process, while the battle for the Brock Field remained a bloody stalemate.

Palmer's other two brigades met the enemy in the woods and formed a line facing southeast. Just behind them ran a little dirt track known locally as the Brotherton Road, after the farmer whose cabin stood at the road's intersection with the La Fayette

William B. Hazen: born Vermont 1830; as a child, Hazen moved with his family to Ohio; graduated from the U.S. Military Academy in 1855 twenty-eighth in his class of thirty-four, he entered the 8th Infantry as 2d lieutenant; he served in California and in Texas, where he was wounded in an 1859 engagement with Comanches; promoted to 1st lieutenant in April 1861 and captain the following month, Hazen entered the volunteer army in October 1861 as colonel of the 41st Ohio Infantry; he commanded a brigade in the Army of the Ohio at Shiloh, in the Kentucky Campaign, and at Stone's River; promoted to brigadier general, U.S. Volunteers, in April 1863 (to rank from November 1862), Hazen led a brigade in the Army of the

Cumberland in the Tullahoma Campaign, at Chickamauga, Chattanooga, Knoxville, and in the Atlanta Campaign; during the siege of that city, in August 1864, he assumed command of the Second Division, Fifteenth Corps, Army of the Tennessee, which he led for the balance of the campaign, during the "March to the Sea," and in the Carolinas Campaign of 1865; promoted to major general, U.S. Volunteers, in April 1865, Hazen took command of the Fifteenth Corps in May; brevetted through major general U.S. Army, he continued in the regular army as colonel of the 38th Infantry, transferring to the 6th Infantry in 1869; during this period Hazen distinguished himself as an Indian fighter, becoming one of the frontier army's finest commanders; he also helped expose corruption that resulted in the ouster of Secretary of War William Belknap and served as an observer during the Franco-Prussian War; in 1880 Hazen was named chief signal officer and head of the Weather Bureau with the rank of brigadier general; he was reprimanded for criticism of Secretary of War Robert Lincoln's failure to relieve A. W. Greeley's marooned arctic expedition, which technically came under Hazen's direction; General Hazen died while on active duty at Washington, D.C., in 1887.

Road. The division's right, approaching to within a few hundred yards of the La Fayette Road, lay in some of the battlefield's thickest underbrush. For perhaps a quarter-mile east of the La Fayette Road and from the Brotherton Road several miles southward, dense blackjack thickets reduced visibility in the woods to no more than fifty yards, often much less. In this case, the heavy growth worked to the Federals' advantage, as Cheatham's left-flank brigade fell into confusion, nearly came apart before even making contact with the enemy, and finally blundered up with its flank against the Federal line—with predictable results.

The next troops Rosecrans sent in were those of the third of

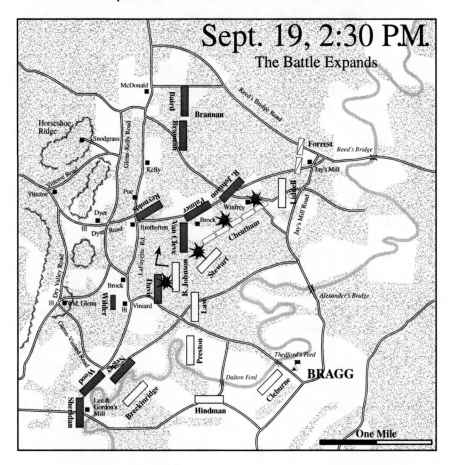

Sept. 19, 2:30 P.M.
The Battle Expands

One Mile

Thomas's divisions, Major General Joseph Reynolds's, finally
finishing the march begun the night before. Reynolds's two
brigades, as well as his steady, competent direction as senior
officer on this part of the front, provided a welcome buttress-
ing for the line along Brotherton Road. It was one of his
brigades that spelled and supported Hazen in the furious
struggle for the Brock Field. Extending the line further south
from the positions held by Reynolds and Palmer was another
of Crittenden's divisions, that of Major General Horatio Van
Cleve. Van Cleve's line formed an angle with that of Palmer,
facing due east and deployed along a slight ridge that ran
through the tangled woods some 300 yards east of the La
Fayette Road, which Rosecrans was determined to hold at all
costs.

The angle in the line gave Van Cleve's men an opportunity
to fire into the flank of the Confederates attacking Palmer's
line, and they made the most of it, helping to complete the
wrecking of that end of Cheatham's Division. With Cheatham in
deep trouble, and a gap threatening to open between him and
the corps of Major General John B. Hood further south, Bragg
yanked Major General Alexander P. Stewart's Division out of
its reserve position in Buckner's Corps and sent it in on
Cheatham's left. Stewart was still relatively new to division
command. Uncertain of himself, he wanted Bragg to give him
precise directions. These Bragg could not give, since he had no
precise information in this most confused of battles. Stewart
would just have to make the best of whatever his skirmishers
flushed out of the smoke-filled, shell-splintered woods toward
the La Fayette Road.

He got off to a rough start. Just getting a divisional line
pointed in the right direction in such a forest proved to be far
from a straightforward proposition. The resulting confusion created a situation in which only a single of Stewart's brigades,
three Alabama regiments under Brigadier General Henry D.
Clayton, actually struck Van Cleve's line head-on, while the other

two brigades came up behind Cheatham and had to be warned by his officers that they were in some danger of being enfiladed. Alone against Van Cleve, Clayton's Alabamians never had a chance. Van Cleve's two front-line brigades overlapped them on both flanks, and the men of Palmer's Division, now relieved of any pressure from Cheatham, gleefully returned the favor Van Cleve's men had done them a few minutes before by pouring a devastating enfilade fire into the Alabamians' flank. Back went Clayton's line.

Stewart was not finished yet, however, and got a brigade of Tennesseeans under Brigadier General John C. Brown into the fight. At first the results were no better. Then the momentum began to shift.

The key to this shift was the fact that in all the confusion and the shuffling of divisions from different corps past and around each other and up the La Fayette Road, Rosecrans had gotten his army tangled up with itself, and south of Van Cleve a yawning gap in the Union line left a half mile of countryside devoid of Union troops. Ordinarily an error such as this would have been obvious to both sides, but in these woods and thickets, officers could only stumble on the truth.

Van Cleve knew at least that he was not in contact with friendly forces on his right and tried to remedy the situation by moving up his reserve brigade to extend his line in that direction. For perhaps half an hour of furious fighting, as the division threw back the attacks of Stewart, that served the purpose. Then affairs took a decided turn for the worse. The new right-flank brigade had tried so hard to make contact with Union forces on the right that it had left a gap between itself and the rest of Van Cleve's division on its left. As the Rebels began to pour through that breach, something far worse happened on the right. Colonel John S. Fulton's Brigade of Tennesseeans, part of Bushrod Johnson's Division, drove right into the 600-yard gap remaining on Van Cleve's right. The truth of the situation began to dawn on Fulton as he drove deep into the Federal position without encountering resistance. Wheeling his brigade to the north, he came crashing onto Van Cleve's flank and crumpled up the whole division. The Federals fled back across the La Fayette Road, some brigades not regrouping until they had fallen back a half mile. With such reserves as were on hand, along with what troops they could rally, Reynolds and Van Cleve managed to patch together a line just west of the La Fayette Road.

While the east side of the La Fayette Road along this stretch was a dense thicket and tangle of vines, the west side was Farmer Brotherton's long rectangular cornfield, stretching about 600 yards along the road and perhaps 150 back from the road to the western woodline. Parallel to the road and running down the middle of the field for its whole length was a substantial ridge, along whose crest much of the reserve artillery of several divisions, twenty guns in all, was deployed. The position had serious drawbacks as a main line of resistance, but for the moment it was the best available to the Federals without falling back far to the west. The stand would have to be made here. It was 4 P.M. now, and a very brief lull descended on this part of the field. In the dense underbrush beyond the La Fayette Road, the Rebels were stirring, obviously preparing to renew the assault. Yet as silence fell over the open ridge and the blood-drenched woods beyond, the soldiers on this part of the front might well have heard for the first time the roar of battle that had for two hours been throbbing over the woodlands from about half a mile to the south on the La Fayette Road. The rest of the army was engaged. The men on the ridge would have had leisure no more than to take note of the fact as they bit off the ends of paper cartridges, rammed the loads home in their rifles and prepared to meet the next Confederate rush.

3

A DEEP, STEADY THUNDER

Rosecrans had been spending most of his time at his new headquarters, the house of a widow named Eliza Glenn on a prominent hill several hundred yards west of the La Fayette Road and south of the Brotherton Field. Regardless of the elevation, he could see nothing beyond the confines of the Glenn Field, rolling downward from the house to the La Fayette Road. Instead, he had been following the progress of the fighting by sound. As things had heated up in the Brotherton Road-Brotherton Field sector about noon, Rosecrans had become absorbed with the fighting there and had given little attention to what was taking place on his right. By late afternoon he would not be able to ignore it any longer.

Rosecrans had been shifting troops up from the army's old position around Lee and Gordon's all day. When the division of Brigadier General Jefferson C. Davis had come up early that afternoon, the army commander could give only very imprecise orders for the very good reason that what he knew of the battle was based mostly on what his ears could tell him of distance and direction. To Davis he recommended the same method of operations. The division commander was to take his division toward the sound of the heaviest firing and try to turn the Confederate southern flank, wherever that might be. Davis brought his division aggressively forward and across the La Fayette Road, but orienting on battle sounds in a thick wood-

Jefferson C. Davis: born Indiana 1828; Davis fought in the Mexican War as a teen-aged volunteer; commissioned into the regular army as 2d lieutenant of artillery in 1848, gaining promotion to 1st lieutenant in 1852; he was on duty during the bombardment of Fort Sumter in April 1861; promoted to captain in May, Davis entered the volunteer army in August as colonel of the 22d Indiana Infantry, with which he fought at Wilson's Creek, Missouri; promoted to brigadier general, U.S. Volunteers, to rank from December, he led a division at Pea Ridge, Arkansas, in March 1862

and at Corinth, Mississippi; in September 1862 at Louisville, Kentucky, Davis initiated an altercation with his superior, General William "Bull" Nelson, in which Davis shot and killed Nelson, reportedly in cold blood; no charges were ever filed and Davis returned to duty, commanding a division in the Army of the Cumberland at Stone's River, Chickamauga, and during the Atlanta Campaign; in August 1864 he assumed command of the Fourteenth Corps, with the brevet rank of major general, U.S. Volunteers; he led the corps with distinction for the remainder of the Atlanta Campaign, in General William T. Sherman's March to the Sea, and in the Carolinas Campaign of 1865; brevetted through major general, U.S. Army, Davis never received promotion to the full rank of major general of volunteers, for which he was entitled and repeatedly recommended; although embittered by this perceived injustice, he continued in the regular army as colonel of the 23d Infantry, exercising departmental command in Alaska and participating in the campaign against the Modoc Indians in California; General Davis died at Chicago in 1879. Although his killing of General Nelson doubtless affected his promotion and likely prevented a more prominent role in the post-war army, Davis was a competent and often outstanding officer.

land was notoriously difficult. So it was that Davis's Division advanced well to the south of Van Cleve's position, leaving that unfortunate half-mile gap that was presently to cause so much trouble up the line in the Brotherton Field sector.

Instead of extending Van Cleve's line, Davis got into his own nasty little fight just east of the La Fayette Road and north of a large field belonging to a farmer named Viniard. Davis took just two brigades into battle, the other having been left behind to cover the wagon trains. His lead brigade was commanded by Colonel Hans Heg, a Norwegian-American from Wisconsin. Besides Heg's own 15th Wisconsin, the brigade included the Army of the Cumberland's only Kansas regiment along with two from Illinois. Crossing the Lafayette Road near a little log schoolhouse about 2 P.M., the Westerners shouldered their way into the vines and scrub oak beyond. They had gone several hundred yards when they suddenly encountered Confederates in line of battle at deadly range. Each line loosed a deadly volley almost into the faces of the other. Then, as one of their officers remembered, the soldiers rammed down loads and blazed away at each other "with an earnestness and deadly furor that I have never seen equalled."

These Southerners were Tennesseeans of Bushrod Johnson's Division, extending the Confederate line southward from Stewart's position. Surprised by this assault, the Rebels nevertheless gave back as good as they got, and Johnson soon had the divisional artillery in action too. "At once," recalled one of Heg's Kansans, "the roar of battle became one steady, deep, jarring thunder." Men on each side remembered the action as among their most intense experiences of combat during the war. Each side began to take alarming losses, but the Confederates, with the advantage of numbers, could better afford them. Gradually Heg's men began to fall back.

At 2:30 Bragg ordered corps commander John B. Hood to find and crush the Federal southern flank in order to relieve the pressure on Stewart and Cheatham farther north. Hood

John Bell Hood: born Kentucky 1831; Hood was graduated from the U.S. Military Academy in 1853, forty-fourth in his class of fifty-two that included Philip Sheridan, James B. McPherson, and John M. Schofield; commissioned 2d lieutenant, he served on the frontier most notably with the elite 2d Cavalry, a regiment that included Robert E. Lee, Albert Sidney Johnston, William J. Hardee, George H. Thomas, and many other future Civil War generals; while on duty in Texas, Hood was wounded in an engagement with Comanches; he resigned his 1st lieutenant's commission in 1861 to enter Confederate service at the same grade; he rose quickly through the ranks to major, commanding all cavalry at Yorktown; in October 1861 Hood became colonel of the 4th Texas Infantry; promoted to

brigadier general in March 1862, he commanded the Texas Brigade during the Peninsular Campaign and the Seven Days Battles, during which the brigade spearheaded the Confederate breakthrough at Gaines' Mill; Hood commanded a division at Second Manassas, again delivering a crushing attack, and at Sharpsburg (Antietam), where his division was sacrificed to buy time for Lee's army; promoted to major general, he led his division at Fredericksburg and at Gettysburg, where a wound rendered his left arm virtually useless; returning to duty, he commanded General James Longstreet's Corps in the Confederate breakthrough at Chickamauga but was again wounded, losing his right leg; promoted to lieutenant general in February 1864 (to rank from September 1863), he joined the Army of Tennessee in March; he directed a corps during the Atlanta Campaign until selected to replace General Joseph E. Johnston with the temporary rank of full general; he fought a series of battles around Atlanta but was forced to evacuate that city on September 1, 1864; leading his army into Tennessee, he fought a bloody battle at Franklin in November and was routed at Nashville the following month; relieved at his own request in January 1865, he surrendered at Natchez, Mississippi, in May; after the war he engaged in business in New Orleans, married, and fathered eleven children; General Hood died at New Orleans along with his wife and eldest daughter during the yellow fever epidemic in 1879. As a combat commander, Hood was unsurpassed; he ranks among the best brigade and division commanders in the war. While not ideally suited to corps or army command, he performed credibly during the Atlanta Campaign; the utter failure of his Tennessee Campaign severely tarnished an otherwise stellar career.

ordered Johnson to wheel to his right, but since Johnson was already heavily engaged with Heg, the result was less than anticipated. One and a half of Johnson's brigades made the wheel and helped break Van Cleve's line. The other brigade and a half found it impossible to disengage in front and so kept on pressing Heg. The Norwegian, in turn, finding the pressure eased, dug in his heels and stopped the Confederate advance.

Back on the La Fayette Road, General Crittenden had taken the situation in hand. Though Davis's Division did not belong to his corps, this battle was not being fought by corps but by miscellaneous collections of detached divisions and even brigades. That was Rosecrans's doing. With no corps to command, Crittenden turned his attention to the fighting in the Viniard Field sector, and since Rosecrans seemed inclined to ignore that front, it was a very good thing he did. Taking stock of the forces available to support Heg, Crittenden found he had Davis's other brigade, that of Brigadier General William P. Carlin, and also, most providentially, Wilder's Lightning Brigade with its fearsome Spencers, holding log-and-rail breastworks in the woods at the far west edge of the Viniard Farm, about 400 yards west of the La Fayette Road. Crittenden sent Carlin in on Heg's right, advancing through the open Viniard Field. Wilder he inserted on the left, dismounted. The reinforced Federal battle line rolled forward again.

Once again the Union advantage proved short-lived. As part of his effort to turn the Federal right, Hood followed up Johnson's Division with that of Brigadier General Evander M. Law. This was the division Hood himself had brought down from Virginia and included the Texas Brigade at the head of which Hood had first achieved glory at such fields as Gaines Mill and Antietam. The Texans were now led by Brigadier General Jerome Robertson, but had lost none of their pride. Johnson's men had taken the very sensible step of loading and firing from a prone position. As the Texans' line swept forward past the Tennesseeans, one of Robertson's men called out,

"Rise up, Tennessee, and see Texas go in!" If the Tennesseeans made any reply at the moment, no one thought to write it down. Apparently Johnson's men were content to let Crittenden's bluecoats make their point for them.

At first Law's men had things pretty much their own way, but when Robertson's men moved to threaten one of the Federal batteries supporting Carlin's Brigade, they ran into trouble. Wilder, who had moved his brigade back into its supporting position, saw the danger and swung two regiments out to counter it. The rapid fire of the Spencers drove the Texans back in disorder. As they passed Johnson's line heading the other way, a waggish Tennessean called out, "Rise up, Tennessee, and see Texas come out!"

The fight around the Viniard Field was far from over, though. Both of Hood's divisions regrouped and continued to press Davis's Federals. When that force proved too little, Hood asked Bragg for reinforcements and got one brigade of Preston's Division. Crittenden, in turn, got a detached brigade of Van Cleve's Division (one that had not joined the fighting around Brotherton Field), and then the division of Brigadier General Thomas J. Wood, but as the battle raged back and forth through the woods and the open Viniard Field, the Confederates increasingly got the advantage. Several times Wilder alertly swung all or part of his Lightning Brigade into action to break up Confederate attacks that threatened to flank Crittenden on either side or to split his line.

Still the Federal position became increasingly desperate. Carlin was forced back on his gun line, along a slight rise just east of the La Fayette Road. Heg's men hung on grimly in the woods fringing the east side of the road just north of them, and a handful of men from the 15th Wisconsin holed up in the log schoolhouse and made Robertson's resurgent Texans pay a high price to take them. Finally, though, the pressure was too great, and the survivors of Davis's Division broke and fled across the La Fayette Road, through the Viniard farmstead and finally took shelter in a shallow streambed or drainage ditch about a hundred yards west of the road. Heg tried to rally them but fell, mortally wounded. Dozens of Union soldiers were shot down like so many cattle as they crowded up against the Viniards' barnyard fence in their flight from the pursuing Rebels. To the left of Davis's position Confederates surged across the La Fayette Road and into the Glenn Field. For Rosecrans the seriousness of the situation was underscored when his own headquarters at the Widow Glenn's came under fire and he had to make a hasty shift to safer parts.

Carlin, Davis, and Crittenden hoped to make a stand in the dry creekbed, but it was no use. The men were exhausted and demoralized, and when the Confederates continued to press the attack, they fled the creekbed and dashed toward Wilder's position at the far west edge of the field. Years later Sergeant Benjamin McGee of Wilder's Brigade remembered how the fugitives "reached our works and poured over them like sheep in a panic." Then McGee relived in mind the tension of those few intense moments: "We know the Rebels will be upon us in a few minutes. It is the supreme moment that tries every man's soul and tests the courage of the stoutest hearts. Panic is infectious, and generally spreads like fire in dry straw. Davis's panic stricken troops are clambering over our works of rails and logs and stumbling over us in wild confusion, many of them wounded and bedrabbling us with their hot, dripping blood." Then as the Confederates attempted to follow, Wilder's men cut loose a rapid and accurate fire, devastating the charging Rebels. "In two minutes," McGee wrote, "there is not a man...seen upon his feet in our front." The Confederates fled back to the creekbed.

To dislodge them from that position, the enterprising Wilder contrived to get his attached artillery battery around on his left front, supported by his Spencers, and blast double and triple loads of canister right down the length of the creekbed packed full of Rebels. The slaughter surpassed all the horrific butchery that had gone before. "It actually seemed a pity to kill men so," Wilder wrote. "They fell in heaps; and I had it in my heart to order the firing to cease, to end the awful sight." He did not have to; the surviving Confederates streamed back across the La Fayette Road in retreat.

By now it was near sundown, and the arrival of another division of Federals moving up from Lee and Gordon's Mill solidified Union control of the Viniard Farm as fighting closed for the night.

Meanwhile back at the Brotherton Field, another crisis had been met and passed. The lull around 4 P.M. had ended abruptly as Stewart hurled his division, now regrouped, right at the angle of the Federal line where the Brotherton Road met the La Fayette Road. Three Confederate attacks had already broken against this section of line, but this time it was different.

For one thing, the ridge in the Brotherton Field was a deceptively weak defensive position. Too close to the thick woods east of the La Fayette Road to allow a good field of fire, it presented its defenders skylined on its crest with no cover but the corn stubble. For another, the troops defending it were fought out after their unpleasant encounter with Johnson's Division, and those Confederates were still plaguing their right flank, now working their way into a wooded ravine on the south edge of the field from which they picked off the crews of the Federal guns on the ridge. Finally, this attack included a fresh brigade led by one of the fightingest men in the Army of Tennessee.

Brigadier General William B. Bate was a hard-charging, ambitious, intensely driven man not always very pleasant to be around but handy to have in a fight. As his brigade prepared to advance this afternoon, he had braced up his regimental commanders to a high pitch of aggressiveness. "Now Smith," he roared to Colonel Thomas Smith of the 20th Tennessee as he reined up, "Now, Smith, I want you to sail on those fellows like you were a wildcat."

Just after four o'clock, Stewart's attack went in, and Bate and his brigade sailed on their hapless opponents like a whole army of wildcats. Van Cleve's line went to pieces at both ends and the middle all at once. Clayton's and Brown's brigades pursued it straight west, through the Brotherton Field, through the woods on the other side, out into the Dyer Field beyond, and toward the Dry Valley Road—the last possible Federal line of retreat now that the La Fayette Road was lost. There, however, they ran out of steam. Rosecrans had reserves coming up in timely fashion. Negley's division, finally making the march the rest of Thomas's men had made the night before, appeared

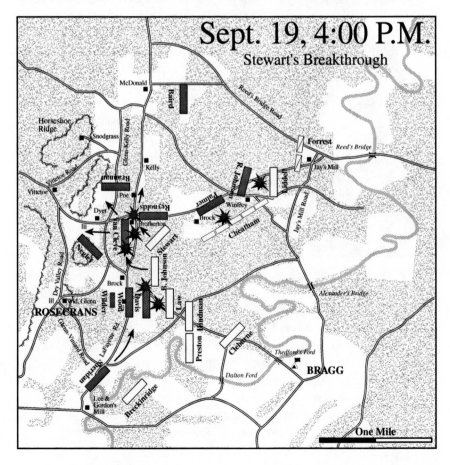

Sept. 19, 4:00 P.M.

Stewart's Breakthrough

One Mile

at the ideal moment, and the potentially deadly Confederate thrust was blunted.

Meanwhile Bate had angled his wildcats more to the right, bearing northward up the La Fayette road, fighting hard and threatening to roll up the whole Federal line north of the Brotherton Road. Reynolds saw the danger and acted quickly

Alexander P. Stewart: born Tennessee 1821; Stewart was graduated from the U.S. Military Academy in 1842, twelfth in his class of fifty-six; commissioned 2d lieutenant and posted to artillery, he saw garrison duty and taught at the academy; he resigned his commission in 1845 to teach mathematics and philosophy at Cumberland University and the University of Nashville; although an anti-secessionist, Stewart offered his services to the Confederacy, becoming a major of artillery; after seeing action in Kentucky and Missouri, he was appointed brigadier general in November 1861; he led a brigade at Shiloh, Perryville, Murfreesboro, and in the Tullahoma Campaign; elevated to major general in June 1863, Stewart commanded a division at Chickamauga, where he was slightly wounded, and at Chattanooga; during the Atlanta Campaign he assumed command of the Army of Mississippi (redesignated Stewart's Corps, Army of Tennessee) upon the death of General Leonidas Polk in June 1864; promoted to lieutenant general, Stewart led his corps with great distinction throughout the balance of the campaign, most notably at Peachtree Creek on July 20; he was also wounded in the ill-advised action at Ezra Church on July 28; Stewart became a true stalwart during General John B. Hood's disastrous Tennessee Campaign after which he joined General Joseph E. Johnston's command in North Carolina, where he surrendered what remained of the Army of Tennessee in April 1865; following the war, he returned to teaching and engaged in the insurance business; in 1874 he was named chancellor of the University of Mississippi, a position he held until 1886; he later became commissioner of the Chickamauga-Chattanooga National Military Park; he died at Biloxi, Mississippi, in 1908. General Stewart was among the Confederacy's most competent Western Theater commanders, participating in almost every battle fought by the Army of Tennessee.

to meet it, as did Hazen. Both of them gravitated to the Poe Field, the next clearing up the La Fayette Road from the Brotherton farm, about 300 yards away. Stretching about another 400 yards along the east side of the road, the Poe Field seemed to offer the best chance of stemming the Confederate tide. Desperately Reynolds and a few staff officers worked to patch together at the north end of the field a line of infantry out of bits and pieces of various regiments and brigades, while Hazen devoted himself to assembling some twenty guns from four different batteries. So absorbed was the brigadier in this activity that he failed to notice Reynolds bringing up two fugitive regiments of Hazen's own brigade. Hazen would later report that he had been the only general officer in the area at the time and that no more than two minutes passed from the time he got there until the Confederates struck, an impossible time span for all that happened.

Addled Hazen might have been, but he got the guns in line and was ready when Bate's yelling Tennessee wildcats charged out of the woods 350 yards distant at the south end of the field. Hoping to keep the momentum of his attack going, Bate was pushing on without support. The question now was whether the Union line at the north end of the field had the firepower and the willpower to stop him. The answer took little more than three minutes to convey. As the Rebels charged into the field, the Federal batteries opened with a deafening roar and choking clouds of sulfurous white smoke. The range was perfect for the Civil War cannon's most deadly ammunition—canister. This load was, in effect, a bucket of musket balls that scattered on leaving the muzzle and turned each cannon into a gigantic sawed-off shotgun. The gunners knew their business and were aiming low, skipping thousands of lead slugs off the ground just in front of—and directly into—the charging Confederates, raising a thick cloud of yellowish dust to mix with the white gunsmoke. "When all was over, and the dust cloud had lifted," wrote one of Hazen's staff officers, "the spectacle was too dreadful to describe. The Confederates were still there—all of them, it seemed—some almost under the muzzles of guns. But not a man of all these brave fellows was on his feet, and so thickly were all covered with dust that they looked as if they had been reclothed in yellow." Almost miraculously,

Patrick R. Cleburne: born Ireland 1828; served for three years in the British Army before purchasing his discharge and migrating to the United States in 1849; settling in Helena, Arkansas, he became a naturalized citizen; worked as a druggist and studied law, gaining admittance to the bar in 1856; in 1860 he helped organize a local militia company, the Yell Rifles, and became its captain; with the secession of Arkansas, Cleburne was elected colonel of a regiment that eventually became the 15th Arkansas; joined General William J. Hardee's command in the advance on Bowling Green, Kentucky, beginning a long association and friendship with that

officer; promoted to brigadier general in March 1862, Cleburne led a brigade with conspicuous skill at Shiloh; commanding a provisional division, he was instrumental in the Confederate victory at Richmond, Kentucky, where he was shot through the face; back with his brigade, he was again wounded at Perryville in October 1862; promoted to major general in December 1862, he led a division at Murfreesboro and Chickamauga; his command held its position on Missionary Ridge during the rout of General Braxton Bragg's Army of Tennessee and then covered Bragg's retreat; his stand at Ringgold Gap may have saved the army from destruction; his off-the-battlefield actions, however, cost him further promotion; he was an ardent member of the anti-Bragg faction calling for that general's removal and his proposal to arm slaves for service in the Confederate Army angered many, including President Jefferson Davis; Cleburne fought throughout the Atlanta Campaign, but was continually passed over for promotion; he was killed during the savage fighting at Franklin, Tennessee, in November 1864. General Cleburne was arguably the finest general officer in the Army of Tennessee and among the best to emerge during the war. He was one of only two foreign-born officers to become a major general in the Confederate Army.

Bate and just over two-thirds of his men had made it back to Confederate lines.

Stewart's assault, full of promise for the Confederates and threatening disaster for the Federals, had spent itself at last. Nightfall was coming on, yet one act remained in the day's fighting. Bragg brought up Cleburne's Division in support of Cheatham's exhausted right flank brigades. Cleburne was by far the best division commander in the Confederate Army and had made his division one of the best too. His three brigades struck the fought-out Federals of Johnson's and Baird's Divisions just as they were about to pull back on Thomas's

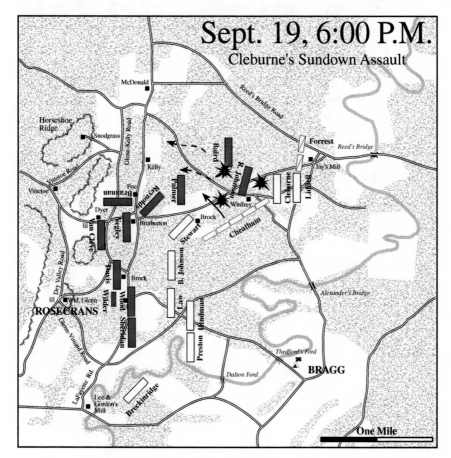

Sept. 19, 6:00 P.M.
Cleburne's Sundown Assault

orders to a superior defensive position. Federals and Confederates shot and stabbed blindly at one another in a brief, vicious, but inconclusive fight amid the gathering darkness.

September 19 had been a day of furious battle, with most of both armies engaged and many units suffering appalling casualties. In the Viniard farmyard and the dry creekbed that ran nearby, around the log schoolhouse just up the road, and in the Brotherton Field, the Poe Field, the Brock Field, and innumerable nameless thickets and woodland glades roundabout, the dead and wounded lay thick that night, and the latter suffered severely as temperatures dropped for another hard frost. The sound of their moans and cries was one their unwounded comrades and foes alike would not soon forget.

Bragg had come near having a substantial portion of his army driven into the Chickamauga around midday, in the defeat of Walker's corps and Cheatham's division. Rosecrans had experienced his own brush with disaster in late afternoon at both the Viniard and Brotherton Fields. Yet the lines had been restored, the gaps plugged, the enemy located, and nothing decided save that another day of battle would follow.

4

THE TIME FOR FIGHTING

That night the high command of each army made its plans
for the morrow. Rosecrans held a council of war with his top
commanders. The army would stay and fight, but as urged by
Thomas, Rosecrans would keep the left flank strong at all
costs. Once again his goal would be holding the La Fayette
Road in order to keep Bragg from getting between the Federals
and Chattanooga. Thomas's command, three divisions of his
own corps plus Johnson's Division of the Twentieth Corps and
Palmer's of the Twenty-first, would hold a rough semi-circle in
the woods east of Kelly Field. The rest of the army, jumbled
together regardless of corps organization, would close up on
Thomas's right, abandoning Lee and Gordon's Mill and gradually easing back and to the north. The business settled, the
meeting nevertheless continued, the generals behaving char-
acteristically. Rosecrans gabbed, McCook entertained his fel-
low officers with a song, and Thomas snoozed. After the gener-

als finally parted in the wee hours of the morning, Rosecrans sought no sleep but paced up and down in front of his headquarters, sipping tea and munching hardtack.

Across the lines, Bragg was having difficulty with the high command of the Army of Tennessee—as usual. That night the remainder of the reinforcements from Virginia arrived, and with them came Lieutenant General James Longstreet.

James Longstreet: born South Carolina 1821; graduated U.S. Military Academy fifty-fourth in his class in 1842; appointed a brevet 2d lieutenant in the 4th Infantry the same year; promoted to 2d lieutenant in the 8th Infantry in 1845, and to 1st lieutenant in 1847; won brevet promotions to captain and major for gallant conduct in the battles of Contreras, Churubusco, and Molino del Rey during the Mexican War; served as

regimental adjutant from 1847 to 1849; promoted to captain in 1852 and to major (paymaster department) in 1858; appointed Confederate brigadier general, served at First Manassas, and promoted to major general in 1861; distinguished service during Peninsular Campaign, Second Manassas, Sharpsburg, and Fredericksburg in 1862; promoted to lieutenant general in 1862, "Old Pete" became General Lee's senior corps commander; on detached service south of the James River in May 1863 thus missing the action at Chancellorsville; commanded right wing of Lee's army at Gettysburg in July 1863; took his corps by rail to Chickamauga, Georgia, in September 1863 to help defeat General William S. Rosecrans, but failed in his attempt to capture Knoxville, Tennessee; returned to Virginia in 1864 in time to participate in the Battle of the Wilderness, where he sustained a critical wound that incapacitated him until late fall; led his corps during closing months of the war in defense of Richmond; surrendered with Lee to Grant at Appomattox Court House; after the war, he settled in New Orleans, became a Republican, and as a state militia officer led black troops against Confederate veterans during Reconstruction disturbances; enjoyed political patronage from Republicans; wrote his war memoirs, *From Manassas to Appomattox*; died at Gainesville, Georgia, in 1904. Lee called Longstreet "my old War Horse." An able battlefield tactician, he was at times stubborn, quarrelsome, and overconfident in his ability as an independent commander.

Although he had graduated near the bottom of his 1842 West Point class, Longstreet considered himself the war's outstanding general. The self-confidence this instilled in him was sometimes beneficial, as when it helped him maintain his unflappable battlefield demeanor. Sometimes, however, that self-con-

Leonidas Polk: born North Carolina 1806; attended the University of North Carolina and then the U.S. Military Academy, graduating eighth in his class of thirty-eight in 1827; brevetted 2d lieutenant and posted to artillery, Polk served only a few months before resigning to study for the Episcopal ministry; ordained a deacon in 1830, he became Missionary Bishop of the Southwest in 1838 and Bishop of Louisiana in 1841; assisted in the establishment of the University of the South at Sewanee, Tennessee; at the outbreak of the Civil War, Polk accepted a major general's commission from his close friend Confederate President Jefferson Davis;

Polk's departmental command consisted of parts of Arkansas and western Tennessee; he committed a disastrous error in violating Kentucky's neutrality by occupying Columbus in September 1861, opening that state to Federal invasion; commanded a corps with gallantry but little skill at Shiloh and in the invasion of Kentucky; promoted to lieutenant general in October 1862, he directed a corps at Murfreesboro and a wing at Chickamauga; his overt criticism of General Braxton Bragg resulted in his banishment from the Army of Tennessee; he was given command of the Department of Alabama, Mississippi, and East Louisiana where he remained until ordered, in May 1864, to join the Army of Tennessee, now headed by Bragg's replacement General J.E. Johnston; Polk led his army (in effect, a corps) during the opening stages of the Atlanta Campaign; on 14 June 1864 he was instantly killed when struck by a solid shot while surveying Federal positions from Pine Mountain near Marietta, Georgia. General Polk's impact on the Confederate cause was largely negative. His violation of Kentucky neutrality proved irreparable and his feud with Bragg severely damaged the effectiveness of the Army of Tennessee. Davis's reluctance to remove Polk only exacerbated the situation.

fidence made him well-nigh unbearable. Of late, Longstreet had entertained notions of replacing the unpopular Bragg, commanding the Army of Tennessee, and getting out from under what he considered the irritating direction of Robert E. Lee, a general he held to be decidedly his inferior. His desire to supplant Bragg had been largely behind his urging for the very movement he was now making. None of this was auspicious for his relations with Bragg.

Once he got to Georgia, things went from bad to worse. Arriving the evening of September 19 at the nearest railroad station, Longstreet fumed that no one was there to meet him. How could Bragg let a mere pitched battle prevent a proper reception for someone of his importance? Longstreet set out with his staff to ride to Bragg's headquarters, rode into Union lines by mistake, bluffed his way out (Longstreet was an excel-

Daniel Harvey Hill: born South Carolina 1821; graduated twenty-eighth of fifty-six at the U.S. Military Academy in 1842; appointed brevet 2d lieutenant 1st Artillery 1842; transferred to 3rd Artillery 1843; promoted to 2d lieutenant 4th Artillery

1845; 1st lieutenant 1847; served in Mexican War, brevetted captain for gallant conduct at Contreras and Churubusco, and brevetted major for meritorious conduct at Chapultepec; resigned from U.S. Army 1849; professor of mathematics, Washington College, Virginia, 1848–54, Davidson College, North Carolina, 1854–59; he became superintendent of the North Carolina Military Institute at Charlotte from 1859 until the Civil War; elected colonel of the 1st North Carolina Infantry, which in June 1861 he led successfully at Big Bethel, Virginia; promoted to brigadier general, served in North Carolina, and returned to Virginia in 1862 as a major general; fought at Williamsburg, Seven Pines, and won praise from General R.E. Lee for his actions during the Seven Days; appointed commander of Department of North Carolina, but returned to division command in the Army of Northern Virginia

lent poker player), and reached Bragg in the middle of the night in a very ugly frame of mind indeed.

Perhaps it was Longstreet's importance, perhaps his ill-disguised sense of self-importance, or perhaps it was the strong reputation Longstreet had won with Lee directing his movements—at any rate Bragg decided to rearrange the command system of his army in order to provide a position of suitable gravity for the new arrival. The army would now be divided into two wings. Longstreet would command the left wing, with the corps of Buckner and Hood as well as Hindman's Division. The right wing would, of necessity go to the next-ranking officer in the army, and that happened to be Leonidas Polk. His command was to include the corps of Hill and Walker as well as Cheatham's over-sized division.

The plan was to be the same as the day before except now

shortly after Second Manassas; falsely accused of losing the Confederate battle plan in Maryland, he fought aggressively at Sharpsburg; poor health and failure to receive promotion to lieutenant general embittered Hill; he returned to administrative duties in North Carolina until in 1863 he accepted corps command in Braxton Bragg's Army of Tennessee; participated in combat at Chickamauga in September; engaged in bitter quarrel with Bragg in which President Davis favored Bragg and relieved Hill from command. Hill spent the rest of the war trying to clear his record, but could obtain only minor commands; in 1864 served as volunteer aide to General Beauregard; for a few days he commanded a division against Union General David Hunter at Lynchburg, Virginia; in 1865 Hill ended his military career by commanding the District of Georgia, fighting at Bentonville, North Carolina, and surrendering with General Johnston at Durham Station. After the war Hill published *The Land We Love,* a monthly magazine, 1866–69, and *The Southern Home*, during the 1870s; he also wrote a number of articles for Century Company's *Battles and Leaders of the Civil War;* in 1877 he became president of what would become the University of Arkansas; in 1885 he became president of Middle Georgia Military and Agricultural College; he resigned in 1889, dying of cancer in Charlotte on September 24. Contemporaries recognized Hill's "well deserved reputation as a hard fighter," but labelled him "harsh, abrupt, often insulting"—a man who would "offend many and conciliate none." He never resolved his quarrel with Davis and Bragg.

the enemy's position was known and the army would face west rather than south. Once again the goal would be to push Rosecrans away from Chattanooga and into McLemore's Cove. For that purpose, the attack would begin on the right and sweep southward along the line, bending back Rosecrans's left flank. As planned for the nineteenth, each wing was to be arranged in depth, with plenty of reinforcements to exploit success. Polk was to open the ball at "daydawn," as Bragg put it, with his lead corps, that of Hill, stepping off at first light to hit the Federals around Kelly Field.

Somehow this sort of thing never seemed to go right in the Army of Tennessee. Polk and Hill never made contact with each other that night, despite various alleged efforts on both their parts to do so. Hill and both men's partisans would argue for years as to whose fault that was. The fact remained that Polk, who had vital orders to convey to Hill for the preparation of a dawn assault that was key to the entire army's battle plans, went to bed without seeing to it that Hill had received and understood his orders. It was a dereliction of duty hardly to be believed, even for so poor a general as Polk.

The result was that on the morning of September 20, no attack went in at "daydawn" or any time close to it. At about that hour Polk rose and discovered that his cavalier arrangements for notifying Hill the night before had not worked. Since no one seemed to know where Hill was, Polk had a staff officer write out orders directly to Hill's division commanders, Breckinridge and Cleburne, to attack "as soon as you are in position." Then, while Polk should have been seeing to such matters himself, he sat down to take his breakfast. By this time Bragg was furious at yet another flouting of his orders and dispatched a staff officer to Polk's headquarters to find out what the matter was. When that officer returned and reported that he had left the bishop-general placidly savoring his morning repast, the commanding general was livid and set out to see Polk himself. By the time he reached Polk's headquarters, that general had ridden to the front. Bragg followed but was too late to catch him at Cleburne's division, though he found there Cleburne and Hill. On receiving Polk's attack order, Hill had told the bishop he was distributing rations to the men and would not be ready for at least an hour. "Sir," inveighed the well-fed Polk, "this is not the time for eating; this is the time for fighting." Then he had ridden off on some other errand, though no one seemed quite sure what.

Bragg repeated the order to attack at once, but more time was lost while Bragg and Hill handled matters that Polk should have dealt with overnight. Cavalry was brought up to

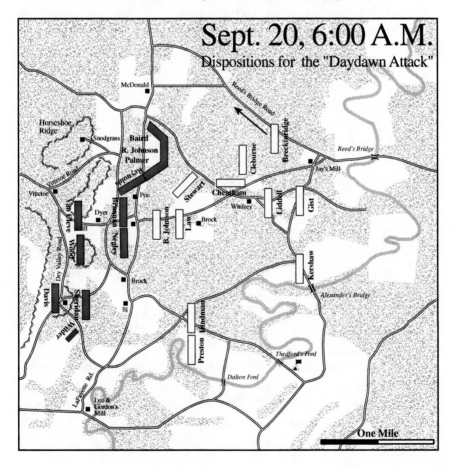

Sept. 20, 6:00 A.M.
Dispositions for the "Daydawn Attack"

One Mile

cover the right flank, and the alignment of Cheatham's division was found to be so hopelessly overlapping Stewart's—indeed, Cheatham's line was perpendicular to his—that Bragg, in despair of getting the units untangled any time soon, simply ordered Cheatham to pull his division back into reserve. Cleburne's and Breckinridge's brigades were aligned as well as time permitted, but Cleburne's division, especially, never really got itself untangled and properly ordered. The attack that had been ordered for dawn—about 5:45 A.M.—did not go in until 9:30 A.M. All the while, from the woods to the west, came the sound of axes as the Federals worked hard to build log breastworks that would multiply the cost and reduce the chance of success of any Confederate assault.

Across the lines, Thomas's blueclad soldiers in their perimeter around Kelly Field had begun their breastworks around daylight. Thomas had a fairly compact position with a large share of the Army of the Cumberland's manpower, but many of the units he would use as reserves to meet sudden Confederate successes did not arrive in the Kelly Field until several hours after sunrise. A Union division commander who fought all day on Thomas's battle line said after the war that had the Confederates attacked at dawn, "the battle would not have lasted an hour; we would have gone to Chattanooga on the run."

While he waited for the Confederates to get started that morning, Thomas apparently decided that it would be a good idea if he could control the intersection of the La Fayette Road with the Reed's Bridge Road, a good half mile north of his present left flank. To accomplish this goal, he asked Rosecrans for his remaining Fourteenth Corps division. So intense was Rosecrans's anxiety to hold his left flank that day, that he would refuse Thomas virtually nothing he asked. Accordingly orders went out for the division, Negley's, to pull out of line further south and march to Thomas's position. All that took time, however, while Thomas waited impatiently and fretted about the Reed's Bridge Road. When Negley's first brigade arrived, Thomas hastened to stretch it the whole distance from his flank to the crossroads. All would be well, after all, when the rest of the division came up.

It was at this moment, however, that the Confederates finally reached a point of preparation that allowed them to refrain from adding more to the already enormous gift of time they had given the Federals. At 9:30 A.M. Breckinridge's Division, on Hill's flank, the rightmost division in the Army of Tennessee, opened the Confederate assault. Breckinridge, who two and a half years before had been vice president of the

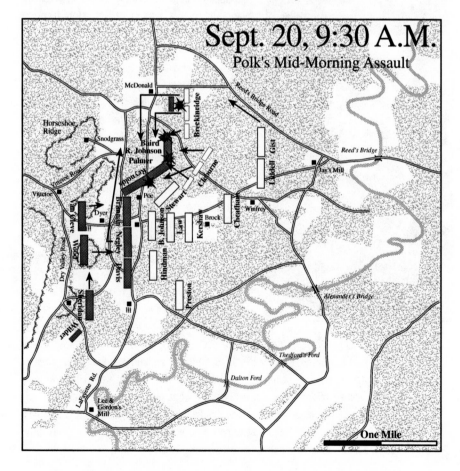

John C. Breckinridge: born Kentucky 1821; member of an old and honored Bluegrass family; attended Centre College, the College of New Jersey (now Princeton), and studied law at Transylvania University; practiced law briefly in Lexington in 1845; after a short residence in Iowa, he returned to Kentucky and married Mary Cyrene Birch; despite his family's Whig background, he took an interest in Democratic politics; saw no action during the War with Mexico, but vis-

ited Mexico City as major in the 3d Kentucky Volunteers; served in the Kentucky legislature from 1849 to 1851, and in the U.S. House of Representatives from 1851 to 1855; nominated and elected Vice President of the United States on the James Buchanan ticket in 1856, the youngest in American history; in 1859, a year and a half before his term was to expire, he was elected to the U.S. Senate by the Kentucky legislature; in 1860 accepted presidential nomination of the Southern Rights wing of the split Democratic Party; favored southern rights, and when Kentucky declared for the Union in September 1861, he accepted a commission as Confederate brigadier general; in 1862 promoted to major general, commanded the reserve corps at Shiloh, defended Vicksburg, and failed in an attack on Baton Rouge, but fought desperately at Murfreesboro; in 1863 participated in General Joseph Johnston's Campaign to relieve Vicksburg; in 1864 commanded the Department of Southwest Virginia, and accompanied General Jubal Early in the raid on Washington; on February 4, 1865, President Davis appointed him secretary of war; following Confederate surrender, he escaped to Cuba, then to England, and finally to Canada; disclaimed all political ambitions, returned to Kentucky, and resumed his law practice. He died in Lexington, Kentucky, in 1875. "What a handsome and imposing appearance he made! Tall, straight, dignified, he was the ideal Kentuckian among Kentuckians," exclaimed a soldier. "Elegantly appareled, wearing the full dress uniform of a Confederate major-general, his bearing was indeed knightly. Boys, he'll do…, ain't he grand?" General Robert E. Lee considered Breckinridge a "lofty, pure, strong man…a great man."

United States, advanced westward with his left flank on the Reed's Bridge Road. His two left brigades never even touched Thomas's main line of resistance as they passed north of it. Instead, they plowed head-on into the single spread-eagle brigade of Negley's division and tore it to pieces.

Reaching the La Fayette Road with two of his brigades, Breckinridge realized he was beyond the Union left flank. He now occupied the position toward which the whole Army of Tennessee had been striving for the last week and a half, and he proposed to make the most of it. Deploying a brigade on either side of the La Fayette Road—and now perpendicular to it—he moved south, toward the flank and rear of Thomas's position around Kelly Field.

Breckinridge's third brigade was not having by any means such an easy time of it. It was the Kentucky Brigade, known affectionately to Breckinridge, himself a Kentuckian, as the "Orphan Brigade," for its men had made a choice different from that of their state. Its commander, Brigadier General Ben Hardin Helm, had a different sort of distinction relative to the executive branch of the U.S. government than did Breckinridge. Helm's wife was a Todd and had an older sister named Mary. Some years past, Mary had wed a lanky Kentucky-born Illinois lawyer, and they now resided in Washington—in the White House.

Helm had a tough task before him. On the left of Breckinridge's line, he was too far south to clear Thomas's main line of breastworks, a fact he discovered only when his line drew fire from them. Unlike Breckinridge's other two brigades, the Orphans were going to have to do some serious fighting before they could see the interior of Thomas's position. From the start, nothing went right for Helm and his Kentuckians. The Federal works curved back toward the west here, and in the woods and smoke and inevitable confusion of battle, half the brigade broke apart from the other and slid off uselessly to the right. To the left, where Cleburne's Division, usually the army's most reliable, should have been adding its weight to the attack, was only the empty forest. Helm, with his remaining regiments, tried again and again to break the Union line, only to be driven back with fearful losses before the rifles and artillery of Thomas's men. Finally, the brigade had spent itself, and Helm was dead, and the Federal line had held.

Cleburne was not really to blame for his division's miserable performance this day. Much of his habitual success as a division commander rested on his meticulous preparation. At sunrise on September 20 his brigades were still for the most part in the positions where they had halted after the previous evening's attack, and Cleburne had no inkling that they were to be called on for early morning work. As a result of Polk's dereliction, Cleburne had to go into battle with the hastiest of preparations. His brigades were not properly aligned and his brigadiers did not fully understand what was expected of them. The advance was a fiasco, as Cleburne's brigades veered off course and became entangled with one another and even with the neighboring troops of Stewart's division, part of Buckner's corps of Longstreet's wing of the army. They blundered into the Federal line one by one, unsupported, sometimes even presenting their flanks to the defensive line as they mistakenly approached it at an oblique angle. Their loss was heavy, including one of the brigade commanders, and the impression they made on Thomas's lines was nil.

Thomas could have rested easy during this attack if not for the fact that Breckinridge had chosen this moment to make his appearance in Kelly Field, squarely in the rear of the Federal battle line. For the Union commander, it was hardly a time to receive visitors, particularly those who came by the back door and gave indication of being as disagreeable as Breckinridge's Confederates had every intention of making themselves.

Moving down the La Fayette Road Breckinridge reached the rear of Thomas's Kelly Field position about 10:30 A.M. Thomas and other Union commanders in the area did their best to react. Union reserves managed to halt Breckinridge's brigade advancing west of the La Fayette Road, but the one on the east side penetrated to the edge of the woods on the north side of the field and opened a withering rifle fire on everything that moved over the broad expanse of corn stubble. That was plenty; staff officers, couriers, and various Union soldiers whose duties took them behind the immediate firing line were scampering hither and yon like ants whose hill had been kicked over. Several of the units drawn up in reserve in the field attempted to answer the Confederate challenge, but the shock of the Southerners' sudden appearance from an unexpected direction, the complexity of changing front to meet them, and the horrifying effect of their rapid rifle fire broke up the Federal reserves and added their numbers to the mob of scattering fugitives. In theory, Thomas had numbers enough to do the job, but for a few minutes it appeared that the lone Confederate brigade might parlay its momentum and the Federals' confusion into a victory against numerical odds.

At this point, Van Derveer's Brigade arrived from a reserve position farther south. The brigade included regiments as different as the Cincinnati Germans of the 9th Ohio and the northwoodsmen of the 2nd Minnesota, but they had been together through the whole war, knew and trusted each other and their commander, and were about to show what could be accomplished by a well-trained body of men who were loyal to each other.

Van Derveer had orders to support Thomas's line, but nobody had bothered to tell him against what. Knowing that Thomas's line faced mostly east, parallel to the La Fayette Road, Van Derveer had his brigade aligned that way when they came out of the woods on the west side of the road, and his left flank regiments came under immediate deadly flank fire from the Rebels in the trees just 200 yards away.

Added to this shock, a harrowing scene met Van Derveer's men as they emerged from the woods, crossed the La Fayette

Road, and entered Kelly Field. Mixing with the thick white powder smoke was the black wood smoke from the blazing Kelly house and barn, near their right flank. Disorganized Union troops were running pell-mell across the field, seemingly in all directions. A deafening din of artillery and small arms fire came not only from the north, where Breckinridge was, but also from the east and south, where the whole semicircle of Thomas's lines was fighting furiously to fend off Cleburne's disorganized but courageous assaults. It was not easy, but Van Derveer determined that the greatest threat lay to the north and ordered his brigade to wheel across the field.

It was a desperate order under the circumstances, but his men responded, left flank coolly marking time on the La Fayette Road while one man after another was shot down by the Confederates in the trees, right flank advancing with long, rapid strides across the field straight into the hail of bullets—"Keep touch of elbows to the left,"—whole line swinging forward like a gate on its hinge, coming parallel to the enemy, still steady and in formation. Now, for the first time, Van Derveer's men leveled their rifles and poured a deadly volley into the Confederates. Breckinridge's line, which had been starting to advance into the field, staggered back into the woods. For perhaps five or ten minutes, Federals and Confederates blazed away at each other across two hundred yards of open field as fast as they could ram the loads down their rifles, aim, and fire. With the Southerners in the trees and Van Derveer's men in the open field, it was an unequal struggle, and casualties mounted fast among the blue-clad ranks.

Then, for Van Derveer's men, discipline gave way to inspiration. From behind them, the men of the 2nd Minnesota heard Colonel August Kammerling of the 9th Ohio shouting commands to his men, as always, in German. The Germans fixed bayonets and strode forward from their position in the second line, passing through the lines of the startled Minnesotans. Then, his front clear, Kammerling shouted again; the long row of bayonets dropped to a level position, the pace changed from walk to run, and a deep, guttural roar rose from 300 throats. The 9th was making another of its impetuous bayonet charges—alone, unsupported, without orders or authorization. In the rest of Van Derveer's brigade, the officers gaped. Then a sergeant of the 2nd Minnesota jumped out in front of his regimental line shouting, "Don't let the 9th Ohio charge alone!" Now it was the Minnesotans' turn to give voice, and they yelled to burst their lungs while they surged forward after the Germans. The officers could only shrug and follow their men.

The whole brigade charged. Elsewhere in Kelly Field, other units rallied and joined the advance. Breckinridge's line disintegrated, and the Union advance became a chase through the woods all the way to the Reed's Bridge Road, half a mile away.

Some days later, Breckinridge reflected bitterly in his report that with timely reinforcements he might have defeated Thomas. The troops were available in Polk's wing of the army, but the bishop-general had gotten only six of his sixteen brigades into action, and of those, three had been Cleburne's, wasted in an ill-planned assault because Polk had not done his homework.

For now, Thomas's Kelly Field position was secure. Two long hours had passed since Breckinridge's men had started the second day's fighting, and it was now not quite 11:30 A.M. From the south, the thunder of battle rolled ominously across the woodlands.

5
A Scene Unspeakably Grand

Bragg's command headaches had not ended when Breckinridge's troops finally opened the battle more than three and a half hours late. Besides the confused and disjointed manner in which the assaults of D.H. Hill's corps were carried out, Bragg had to worry about the fact that Cleburne's division had run afoul of Stewart's, creating confusion that further disrupted the plan of battle. Since that plan called for each division to attack as soon as the division on its right had gone in, the delay kept the whole Confederate line south of Stewart in idleness. On top of that, Stewart's division was part of Buckner's corps, which was part of Longstreet's wing. Thus, the lowest headquarters that commanded both Cleburne and Stewart was Bragg's own. Untangling this mess would have been distressing enough even without the awareness that a part of the army was already engaged and was failing. As Breckinridge's Division was advancing unsupported against the

Federal flank and Cleburne's was coming to grief in front of the Union breastworks, Bragg simply gave the order for every division in the army to advance immediately, without waiting for the unit on its right.

Stewart's men went forward shortly after eleven o'clock, advancing across the Poe Field from east to west, where Bate had attempted it from south to north the afternoon before. The result, however, was not much different. The flat cornfield made an excellent field of fire from any direction. Union lines fronted it on two sides—just behind the La Fayette Road on the west and in the edge of the woods at the north end of the field where the Union lines curved eastward to form Thomas's salient around the Kelly Field. The result was a deadly crossfire that mowed down Stewart's men and sent the survivors reeling back into the woods where their attack had started.

Further down the Confederate line, however, things were shaping up differently. Just to the south of Stewart, Longstreet had arranged the main body of his wing for the assault. As with Polk, Bragg had given Longstreet enough troops to provide ample reserves, a deep attacking column that would not duplicate Stewart's experience on the afternoon of the nineteenth, penetrating the enemy's line but then being driven back for lack of support. Unlike Polk, however, Longstreet got his forces properly deployed. Partly this was because he had more time, partly because Longstreet possessed real and considerable skill in the basic mechanics of moving his units around on the field of battle. If a superior general would provide the overall tactical and strategic scheme—and if Longstreet would follow it—he could be a useful corps commander. Though he had come west in hopes of eventually getting Bragg's job and he tended to take a condescending view of all other generals, including Lee, Longstreet, having been in the Western theater less than twenty-four hours, was not quite ready to start obstructing his commander's orders. So he had ranged his wing in a powerful attacking column. Stewart was its right

Joseph Brevard Kershaw: born South Carolina 1822; studied law; admitted to the bar in 1843; served in the war with Mexico as a lieutenant of the Palmetto Regiment; stricken by fever while in Mexico, but nursed back to health by Lucretia Douglass, whom he had married in 1844; twice elected to the South Carolina legislature; in 1860 was a member of the state's secession convention; elected colonel of the 2d South Carolina Infantry; participated in the Battle of First Manassas; promoted to brigadier general in early 1862, and played a significant part in the operations of both Joseph E. Johnston and Robert E. Lee in 1862; his "gallantry, cool yet daring courage and skill in the management of his troops" won him praise from his division commander; Kershaw participated in the Maryland Campaign and at

Fredericksburg; in 1863, while temporarily detached from Longstreet's Corps, he and his South Carolinians hammered the Federals at Chancellorsville; later that summer Kershaw lost half his command at Gettysburg; in September he and his brigade accompanied Longstreet west in what became an unsuccessful campaign in Tennessee, but won Kershaw promotion to major general; back in Virginia in 1864, he and his division fought gallantly in the Wilderness and at Spotsylvania, Cold Harbor, and Petersburg; later they successfully reinforced Jubal Early's forces in the Valley, but in October suffered a serious defeat at Cedar Creek; returning to the Richmond area, Kershaw fought his last battle in April 1865 at Sayler's Creek, where his division was overwhelmed and he and large numbers of his men were captured; sent to Fort Warren, Massachusetts, he remained a prisoner of war until August. Kershaw resumed his law practice and political career after the war; elected to the state senate, he served as its president pro tem until the imposition of a reconstruction goverment replaced him in 1866; defeated as a Democratic candidate for Congress in 1874, but three years later he became judge of the state's fifth circuit, a position he maintained until 1893, when sickness compelled him to resign; in 1894 President Grover Cleveland named him postmaster of Camden, South Carolina, but Kershaw held this office less than two months, dying on April 13; he is buried in the local Quaker Cemetery. A distinguished historian ranked Kershaw "without peer as a combat leader. He and his commands were always in the forefront of battle, and during their four years of service compiled a record for valor and self-sacrifice that few units, either in blue or gray, could equal, and none surpass."

flank, Hindman its left. In the center was Hood's entire corps, now reinforced by additional troops from Virginia that had arrived just the night before. Leading Hood's Corps would be Bushrod Johnson's Division, two brigades in front, one following in reserve. Behind Johnson was Law, also two brigades up, one back. Then came the two-brigade division of Brig. Gen. Joseph Kershaw. In all, Hood's column included eight brigades ranged in five lines, all under the command of one of the Army of Northern Virginia's hardest-hitting attack leaders, Hood, and arranged by its most experienced battlefield technician, Longstreet. By eleven o'clock it was poised like a javelin aimed at the heart of the Union position.

The grim determination of Longstreet's men as they waited for the order to advance would have been replaced by wild elation if they could have known what was transpiring in the Union lines in front of them.

Rosecrans, by now a bleary-eyed bundle of nerves, was still intensely concerned about his left flank, determined to reinforce Thomas "with the whole army if necessary." With this in mind he began more of the complicated shuffling of divisions that had been his chief activity the day before. In response to requests from Thomas, Rosecrans started Van Cleve north to reinforce him, and ordered Major General Philip Sheridan, commanding the division on the far right of the line, to pull in his two right brigades and send them marching at top speed toward Thomas's position with the third to follow as soon as possible. The extreme Union right flank, represented by Wilder's Lightning Brigade, was now located at the Widow Glenn Hill, and Rosecrans moved his headquarters farther north to the open north end of a knoll that looked down onto the fields, buildings, and orchard of a farmer named Dyer, several hundred yards west of the Brotherton Field.

About 10:30 A.M., just as Thomas was being struck in flank by Breckinridge while engaged in front with Cleburne and before Van Derveer had arrived to turn the tide in Kelly Field, the Fourteenth Corps commander sent yet another and more urgent appeal for troops and also directed the staff officer, his nephew Sanford C. Kellogg, to go directly to General Brannan first and give him orders to bring up his division. Brannan's Division was part of the Fourteenth Corps and, by the arrangement of the previous night's council of war, was to have been held in reserve at Thomas's summons. That morning, however,

Philip Henry Sheridan: born New York 1831; Sheridan's date and place of birth remain matters of speculation; Sheridan himself gave conflicting information; he may have been born in Ireland or aboard ship during his Irish parents' passage to the United States; whatever the case, the family moved to Ohio when Sheridan was still an infant; he entered the U.S. Military Academy with the class of 1852, but dis-

ciplinary problems delayed his graduation by a year; he finished thirty-fourth in the 1853 class of fifty-two that included John Bell Hood, James B. McPherson, and John M. Schofield; after years of service on the frontier with the 4th Infantry, Sheridan was still a 2d lieutenant on the eve of the Civil War; promoted to 1st lieutenant in March 1861 and captain, 13th Infantry, in May, he served as chief quartermaster and commissary for the Army of Southwest Missouri and was detailed to General Henry Halleck's headquarters during the advance on Corinth, Mississippi; in May 1862 he entered the volunteer army as colonel of the 2d Michigan Cavalry and, by July, was promoted to brigadier general, U.S. Volunteers; he commanded an infantry division at Perryville and Stone's River, gaining promotion to major general, U.S.

Volunteers, to date from December 1862; Sheridan's division was routed at Chickamauga in September 1863, but spearheaded the unauthorized assault that drove the Confederates from Missionary Ridge in November; when General Ulysses S. Grant was named overall commander of Union forces and went east to face General Robert E. Lee, he selected Sheridan to lead the Army of the Potomac's Cavalry Corps; throughout the spring and early summer of 1864, Sheridan's troopers duelled with the once-supreme Rebel cavalry with mixed results; he was victorious in the clash at Yellow Tavern, in which Confederate cavalry commander J.E.

unknown to Thomas, Brannan moved up to plug a gap between the divisions of Reynolds and Wood. Nevertheless, Kellogg delivered the order and a skeptical Brannan reluctantly directed his brigade commanders to prepare to pull out of line.

Kellogg arrived at Rosecrans's headquarters and announced his business and what he had done. The commanding general approved the action and promised to support Thomas with the

B. Stuart was mortally wounded; in response to Confederate General Jubal Early's move on Washington, Grant created the Middle Military Division and placed Sheridan in command; Sheridan's Army of the Shenandoah, consisting of two infantry corps and three large divisions of cavalry, defeated Early at Winchester and Fisher's Hill but narrowly escaped disaster at Cedar Creek when the Rebels surprised Sheridan's army during his absence; Sheridan's ride from Winchester to Cedar Creek to rally his men is among the most well-publicized events of the war; during the fall and winter of 1864-1865, in an awesome display of total war, Sheridan's troops laid waste to the Shenadoah Valley, depriving Lee of much-needed supplies and incurring the wrath of Southerners for generations to come; the fiery Sheridan became a national hero; having been promoted to brigadier general in the regular army in September 1864, he became major general in November; in the spring of 1865 Sheridan, with the bulk of his command, rejoined Grant on the Petersburg front and played a pivotal role in the closing stages of the war; given wide discretion, Sheridan's cavalry ran roughshod over the Rebels at Five Forks and Sayler's Creek, finally cornering Lee's army near Appomattox; while extremely successful on the battlefield, Sheridan's abrasive manner and quick temper led to the unfair removal of General G.K. Warren, a controversy that raged for years; immediately after Lee's surrender, Sheridan was dispatched to the south Texas border with Mexico to discourage French intentions in that country; thereafter his heavy-handed conduct as the reconstruction commander of the Fifth Military District (Texas and Louisiana) brought his removal; when Grant became president and William T. Sherman filled his spot as commanding general, Sheridan became lieutenant general; as commander of the Military Division of the Missouri, he was an aggressive prosecutor of the Indian Wars; during this period he was also an official observer of the Franco-Prussian War and supported the creation of Yellowstone National Park; in 1884, on the retirement of Sherman, Sheridan became commanding general; in June 1888 he was awarded his fourth star; General Sheridan died shortly thereafter at Nonquitt, Massachusetts. He remains among the most influential soldiers in the nation's history.

whole army. It occurred to him, however, that if Brannan had moved out of line, a dangerous gap would exist that would need to be filled. He therefore sent a courier galloping off to Wood, commanding on Brannan's right, with an order to "close up on Reynolds as fast as possible, and support him."

Meanwhile, Brannan had thought better of so reckless a course as opening a gap in the line and had countermanded his orders to brigade commanders to withdraw. The division would now stay put until other troops came up in relief. This was the situation around 11:00 A.M. when Wood, with his division along the western edge of the Brotherton Field, received the vague order from Rosecrans. It made no sense at all under the circumstances. "Close up on Reynolds" suggested a sideways move in line, but that was impossible with Brannan in place. To "support" Reynolds, under the circumstances, Wood must needs have pulled out of line and marched northward behind Brannan, leaving a gaping hole. The commanding general could not possibly have intended that, and ordinarily the officer receiving such an order would have acted on that assumption. This officer, however, was Brigadier General Thomas J. Wood, a brilliant forty-year-old Kentuckian, professional soldier, and second cousin of Ben Hardin Helm. Wood had been deeply offended several days earlier when Rosecrans had irritably denounced him in front of his staff for failing to carry out unquestioningly a vague and confusing order. Now Wood was determined not to endure such a humiliation again. If the general commanding wanted unquestioning obedience to garbled orders, he would get it from Thomas J. Wood. Without hesitation, the Kentuckian ordered his brigadiers to pull out of the line.

That took all the more nerve because at the moment his skirmishers were heavily engaged out in the Brotherton Field. On this day the Federal main line of resistance ran not along the crest of the Brotherton Ridge but behind it, along the rail fence at the western edge of the field; it was still not a good

Thomas J. Wood: born Kentucky 1823; Wood was graduated from the U.S. Military Academy in 1845, fifth in his class of forty-one; originally assigned to topographical engineers, he served as a 2d lieutenant in the Mexican War, earning a brevet for Buena Vista; after transferring to the dragoons he saw a variety of duties on the frontier, during the Kansas border wars, and on the Mormon Expedition, achieving the rank of captain, 1st Cavalry, in 1855; in 1861, as Southern officers left the Army in large numbers, Wood rose rapidly through the ranks, becoming major in March, lieutenant colonel in May, and colonel, 2d Cavalry, in November; he had in the meantime been commissioned into the volunteer army as brigadier general in October; he commanded a division in General Don Carlos Buell's Army of the Ohio at Shiloh, in the advance on Corinth, and at Perryville; wounded at Stone's River on the last day of 1862, Wood refused to leave the field until the day's fighting had ended;

he returned to lead his division in the Tullahoma Campaign and at Chickamauga in September 1863, where his prompt execution of an order nearly resulted in the destruction of the Army of the Cumberland; on directions from General William Rosecrans, Wood pulled his division out of line to fill a gap that did not exist thereby creating an actual gap through which the Rebels poured only moments later; Rosecrans lost his job, but Wood was not disciplined and, two months later at Chattanooga, his troops were among those who spontaneously charged up Missionary Ridge, routing the Confederates; Wood led a division with conspicuous skill throughout the Atlanta Campaign and was wounded on September 2 at Lovejoy Station, again refusing to leave the field; returning to duty he led his division at Franklin and directed the Fourth Corps at Nashville; in February 1865 Wood received the well-deserved promotion to major general, U.S. Volunteers; brevetted through major general, U.S. Army, he reverted to his regular rank of colonel; he served in Reconstruction Mississippi until 1868 when he was retired for disability due to wounds with the rank of major general; in 1875 he was permanently retired as brigadier general, U.S. Army; a member of the U.S. Military Academy's Board of Visitors, General Wood remained active in veterans' organizations until his death at Dayton, Ohio, in 1906.

position, but the best available in this sector. A heavy Federal patrol just a few minutes earlier had revealed that the Rebels were present in massive force just across the La Fayette Road. Yet Wood rejected the pleas of his officers and took his division out of line. Further south, Davis recognized the gap this would leave between himself and Brannan and tried to sidestep his division northward to fill it. At approximately 11:10 A.M., his lead brigade, the decimated regiments that Heg had led into the Viniard Woods the day before, was just filing along Wood's abandoned rail fence even as the last of Wood's brigades disappeared into the forest, when the high, keening wail of the

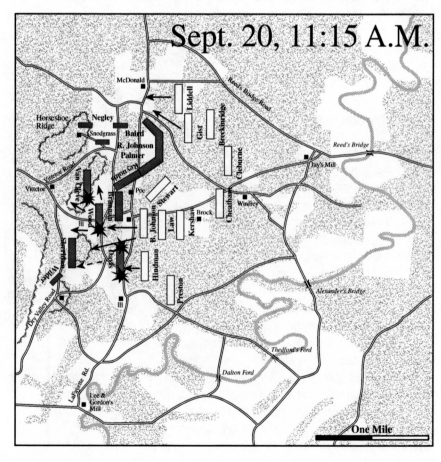

Sept. 20, 11:15 A.M.

Rebel yell rose from the far side of the Brotherton Ridge.

Unwittingly, Longstreet launched Hood's column right at the gap in the Union line. Leading the advance, Bushrod Johnson's men surged over the Brotherton Ridge and downhill toward the woods beyond. The Federals would have been hard put to stop this charge under the best of circumstances, given the fact that only fifty yards separated their line from the first point at which the Confederates appeared along the crest of the ridge. Davis's outnumbered troops, caught out of position, never had a chance. It was a single volley and then the bayonet, and very few of the Federals stayed to try conclusions with the latter weapon. Davis's Division was swept away, as was the trailing brigade of Wood, caught before it could get clear of the oncoming Confederate juggernaut.

Johnson's Confederates rushed on, driving the blue-coated fugitives before them, through the Brotherton Woods some 500 yards, dispersing other Federal units attempting to shore up the nonexistent line. Then it was out into the open field to confront one of the most dramatic panoramas of the war. As they burst out of the woods, the Confederates entered the broad expanse of the Dyer Farm, affording an almost unobstructed view 500 yards deep and more than twice that wide. The far side of the farm sat on a chain of hills that made the giant clearing into a natural amphitheater. "The scene now presented was unspeakably grand," wrote Bushrod Johnson in his report. "The resolute and impetuous charge, the rush of our heavy columns sweeping out from the shadow and gloom of the forest into the open fields flooded with sunlight, the glitter of arms, the onward dash of artillery and mounted men, the retreat of the foe, the shouts of the hosts of our army, the dust, the smoke, the noise of firearms—of whistling balls and grape-shot and of bursting shell—made up a battle scene of unsurpassed grandeur."

In the center of the scene, on an open knoll on the far side of the field, was Rosecrans's headquarters. The general and his staff had been having a few quiet moments just now, and

War Department representative Charles A. Dana had even been dozing on the ground. He awoke with a terrible start to "the most infernal noise I ever heard. Never in any battle I had witnessed," Dana explained, "was there such a discharge of cannon and musketry." The first thing Dana saw when he sat up was the devout Catholic Rosecrans crossing himself. Dana was not encouraged. A staff officer standing beside Rosecrans was hit, and the group hastily mounted up and rode hard for the shelter of the backside of the hill.

The Federals had two chances to contain the Confederate breakthrough. As the Confederates faced the great amphitheater of Dyer Field, those two Federal hopes were units resting on hills on either side of Rosecrans's center-stage position. On a ridgetop to the right of Rosecrans's headquarters, as the Confederates saw it, was a line of artillery pieces that grew by the minute as fugitive guns from the disaster in the center joined up with reserve batteries already positioned there. Soon no less than twenty-nine Federal cannon were thundering their defiance at the Confederates fanning out into the Union rear.

To the other side of Rosecrans's headquarters knoll was an open hill, and on it was drawn up a Federal infantry brigade in battalion column, that is, four regimental battle lines, one behind the other. This was the brigade of Colonel Bernard Laiboldt, of Sheridan's Division, and these Illinoisans and Missourians liked their position. They could deliver devastating firepower in front of them as each regiment fired over the heads of the one in front, further down the slope. Better still, Sheridan's other two brigades were coming up from Widow Glenn's to join them. They felt confident they could maintain their position.

Unfortunately, they were not given the chance to try. At this juncture their corps commander, McCook, happened along. Though a superfluity through the whole battle thus far, McCook unfortunately chose this moment to become relevant. Laiboldt, he ordered, must charge downhill into the maelstrom below and drive the Confederates back to their own side of the Brotherton Woods. Laiboldt remonstrated in vain; McCook would have it no other way. While the soldiers grimly fixed bayonets, McCook rode back to the reverse slope of the hill to join the sheltering Rosecrans and assure him that now all would be well.

He might not have been so glib if he could have seen what was happening on the other side of the hill. Laiboldt's men charged down the slope and into a tanyard with its jumble of shacks and vats. Several times their numbers met them there, lapped around both flanks of each regiment in succession as it advanced, shot down 400 of them, and completed the job of turning a solid and steady veteran brigade into a flock of frightened individuals seeking safety in flight.

Sheridan's other two brigades could have used Laiboldt's help as they were hit in their turn by the tidal wave of Confederate troops. One brigade, that of poet-general William Lytle, took position on the hill Laiboldt had held even as the Confederates who had wrecked Laiboldt's brigade surged up the forward slope. A short, desperate struggle ensued. Lytle, whose poems had charmed the nation, was wounded repeatedly and presently died, while his brigade went to pieces and the victorious Confederates swept onward. The third of Sheridan's brigades, between Lytle's position and the Widow Glenn's, fared little better, and the whole division was routed. Its fragments joined a doleful procession making its way up the Dry Valley Road toward Chattanooga, an appalling jumble of supply wagons, cannon, caissons, and demoralized soldiers, all making the best speed they could in hopes of escaping Confederate pursuit. By this time, the column included Crittenden, McCook, and Rosecrans.

Back out in the Dyer Field the Union guns continued to hammer at the advancing Confederates. Longstreet sized up the situation and realized that until this threat to his right flank was disposed of, he could not afford to set out on the pursuit the beaten Federals dreaded. With that purpose in mind, he ordered his attacking column to wheel to the northward and roll up the Union resistance there.

Commanding the spearhead corps of Longstreet's column, Hood was in his element. "Go ahead, and keep ahead of everything," he told Bushrod Johnson. At the moment, that meant taking those Federal guns on the ridge at the far side of the field, and Hood set out to do just that. While Law's Division charged straight across the open field, Johnson's gained the ridge south of the guns and moved in on their flank. The combination was irresistible. What Union infantry was in line with the guns was in a shaky frame of mind to begin with, being com-

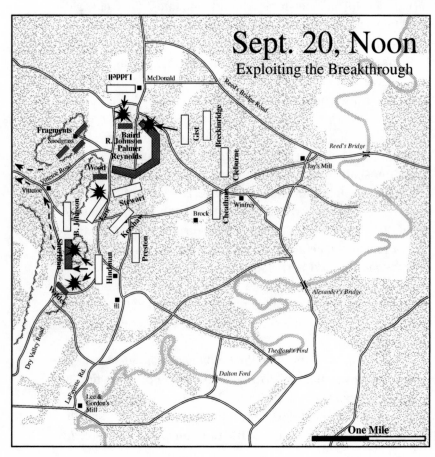

posed of remnants of units blown apart in trying to stop the breakthrough. The blue-coated foot soldiers broke for the rear. The artillerists tried to get their guns off as best they could, but some seventeen of the pieces became prizes of the Confederates.

Hood's orders were the same, and his divisions moved ahead again, still further north through the Dyer Field. As they neared the rail fence that bounded the field on the north, they ran smack into a solid volley of musketry. Obviously, the Union formation along that fence was no mere straggler line. Hood urged his men forward, but even the famed Texas Brigade, Hood's own at the war's beginning, broke under the deadly fire. As Hood rode in to rally them, a bullet slammed into his right leg just below the hip. He was carried from the field still murmuring, "Go ahead, and keep ahead of everything."

The Federals who had shot Hood and wrecked his old brigade belonged to Colonel Charles G. Harker's Brigade of Wood's Division. It had been the first brigade to pull out of line what seemed like an eternity ago but in fact was less than one hour. It had already moved far enough up the line to be clear of Longstreet's attack column, and now Wood, realizing the disaster behind him, had turned it back in hopes of stemming the onrushing Confederates. Harker was a good commander; his men were good soldiers; and for the moment, they did just that.

But Confederate reinforcements were coming up. Even before he fell, Hood had seen the approach of the two brigades of his trailing division, Humphrey's Mississippians and Kershaw's South Carolinians. Now these two brigades in flawless line of battle, their square Army of Northern Virginia battle flags evenly spaced down their front, were advancing through the open field toward Harker's line.

Incredibly, Harker's deadly rifles fell silent, and as the thick white smoke drifted away, the men of each side witnessed another striking panorama. The Confederates saw Harker's line, running from a high hill at the northwestern corner of the field along the far edge to the low ground at the field's north-eastern corner. The Federals crouched silently, almost expec-tantly, as their color-bearers stood at full height and boldly waved the Stars and Stripes back and forth over their heads.

Harker's men themselves were not at all so sure of what they were seeing. The neater uniforms and different style battle flags of these troops from the Army of Northern Virginia looked, from a distance, as if they might belong to Sheridan's or Davis's Division. Up here on the northern flank, the Federals had been hoping that perhaps the divisions at the other end of the army had come through intact, and now it appeared that one of them was approaching. Dreading the thought of firing into friendly troops, Harker and Wood ordered their men to hold their fire while the color-bearers displayed the flags and waited for a reaction. The suspense heightened as the oncoming line closed through prime rifle range.

Harker's men did not have much longer to wait. Kershaw's Brigade opened fire, the Federals gave back as good as they got, and another vicious fight blazed up. It might have had the same result as the one just before save that Kershaw and Humphreys were able to overlap both of Harker's flanks, forcing his brigade to break. Kershaw's jubilant South Carolinians swarmed over the hilltop at the northwest corner of the Dyer Field, then plunged down the farther slope, through scattered trees, to keep up the chase. Harker's men, still full of fight, fell back toward the next ridge to the north, where other refugees of the disaster were forming up around a tiny nucleus of unbloodied units to make a final stand. They drew their line along an open ridge that sloped off from the house of a farmer named Snodgrass.

6
THAT PECULIAR FIERCENESS

The time Harker's men had gained in their stand at the north end of the Dyer Field was just what their comrades on Snodgrass Hill had needed. Brannan was there, and several brigade commanders from the troops that had been routed to the south, and desperately they strove to cobble together a defensive line on the open ridge that ran down to the (Federal) left from the Snodgrass house and on the higher wooded elevations, known as Horseshoe Ridge, that rose to the right of the house. Most important, Thomas was there, taking charge of the defensive arrangements and instilling new confidence into the shocked and skittish troops. Thomas dipped into the reserves he had been holding in Kelly Field, about half a mile to the east, to provide a few unshaken units around which the bits and pieces of the shattered Federal right could form. Those bits and pieces ranged in size from Harker's battered but intact brigade, just falling back to the ridge at 12:45 P.M.

after being forced out of Dyer Field, to the forty or so resolute men who were still around the colors of the 44th Indiana. They were tired, most had already tasted defeat that day, they had no surplus of ammunition, and there were none too many of them in any case. Grimly they awaited Kershaw's onrushing South Carolinians.

The Confederates came on exultantly, expecting to drive the Yankees here as they had in the Dyer Field. They were in for a surprise. The Federal line erupted in volley after volley of musketry. Kershaw's men were driven back; regrouped and came on again; and were driven back the second time. Other

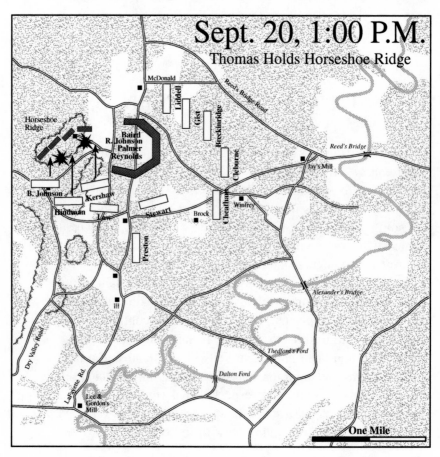

Confederate troops came up and joined in launching repeated attacks at the Snodgrass Hill and adjoining Horseshoe Ridge, but nothing, it seemed, could dislodge the stubborn bluecoats.

Out on the narrow open ridge below the Snodgrass House, Harker was making good use of the terrain. He arranged his brigade in two lines. The first would lie down just behind the crest, while the second took shelter a few yards further down the back slope. When the Confederates advanced, he had the first line stand, loose a volley, and then drop back a few yards down the rear slope to reload in complete shelter while the second line moved up to take their place and deliver its fire. Farther up on Horseshoe Ridge such tricks were not as practical, but the Confederates still had a straight uphill charge against troops who seemed to have found a new source of confidence. It was a confidence that grew as each successive Confederate attack broke up and streamed back to its starting point.

Part of the Confederates' problem was that they could not seem to coordinate their attacks very well. Their efforts to take Snodgrass Hill were brave enough but confused and disjointed. Bragg was counting on Longstreet, the vaunted maker of many a Virginia victory, to direct affairs on this front. Longstreet had been counting on Hood to handle the up-front coordination of the attacks, but up-front coordination of infantry assaults is a dangerous business, and just now Hood was on his way to a field hospital to have his leg amputated. Longstreet knew this, of course, but took no steps to fill the void. By contrast, Thomas, now the senior U.S. officer on the field, established his own headquarters at the most crucial point on what was now his battlefield, a few yards behind the embattled Snodgrass Hill.

But if the Federals, with their inspired leadership and resolute courage, could not be driven off the hill, perhaps they could be flanked off. Bushrod Johnson meant to try, and as he brought up his division, he swung it in on the Confederate left and struck for a point farther up Horseshoe Ridge from where Thomas's men were already fighting for their lives.

In his way, it turned out, were the 539 men of the 21st Ohio. They were veteran troops, and seven of their ten companies carried the strange Colt Revolving Rifle, a five-shot repeater that looked like a revolver sprouted and gone to seed. Still, the odds were extreme against the handful of men from the Buckeye State. The first few assaults they turned back with the firepower of their Colts, and once they even got excited and charged down the rugged hillside after their fleeing attackers—only to run into an even bigger Confederate formation and be forced back up the hill again, losing men at every step. The regimental commander was hit, and his second-in-command took over. Then he went down, and command devolved on a captain. The Rebels kept coming, and as ammunition ran low, men frantically rummaged the cartridge boxes of their fallen comrades. The overheated Colts began to jam. Meanwhile, the Confederates, with their superior numbers, steadily reached farther and farther to the right, up the ridge, and the regiment had to spread out to block them, a single thin line of men, crouching behind rocks and trees, loading and firing, loading and firing.

For both sides the conflict in these bullet-riddled woods had a nightmarish quality. Johnson's men, toiling up the steep hillside, were tired, desperately tired, but they sensed now that total victory was within their grasp, and their equally desperate foes could sense them reaching for it. "There was that peculiar fierceness in the manner of the assault that men show when they realize that the supreme opportunity has presented itself, and are determined not to let it slip," recalled one of the Ohioans, "And our boys could do nothing but set their teeth and fight, as for their lives."

Yet it appeared it would all be for naught. The Confederates finally got on the ridge farther up, on the Ohioans' flank and began to apply pressure there to get the stubborn Buckeyes off

the ridge and get on with rolling up Thomas's last line of
defense. It had almost come to that when Ohioans and
Confederates alike were surprised by a cheer coming from the
back slope of the ridge beyond the Union flank. Then a blue-
clad line of battle crested the ridge and bowled the startled
Confederates right back down the other side.

These were the men of Steedman's Division of the Army of
the Cumberland's Reserve Corps. A small organization of only
three brigades, the Reserve Corps had come into being the
previous summer. Now, commanded by Major General Gordon
Granger, it had been stationed at Rossville, north of the battle-

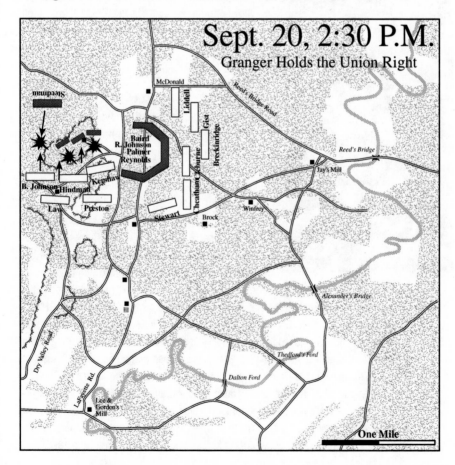

Sept. 20, 2:30 P.M.
Granger Holds the Union Right

field, covering a gap in Missionary Ridge. As Granger heard the sound of fighting to the southward swell to the roar of pitched battle for the second straight day, he decided that his

Gordon Granger: born New York 1822; Granger was graduated from the U.S. Military Academy in 1845 thirty-fifth in his class of fifty-one; originally posted to infantry, he won two brevets during the Mexican War, after which he served on the frontier with the U.S. Mounted Rifles; promoted to 1st lieutenant in 1852, he remained in that grade until the onset of the Civil War; promoted to captain in May 1861 (in August the Mounted Rifles was redesignated the 3rd U.S. Cavalry); during this period he also served briefly as a volunteer lieutenant colonel on the staff of

General George B. McClellan in western Virginia; moving to the Western Theater, Granger worked on Samuel Sturgis's staff at Wilson's Creek, Missouri, in August 1861, after which he was appointed colonel 2d Michigan Cavalry; promoted to brigadier general in March 1862, he commanded the Cavalry Division, Army of the Mississippi, at New Madrid, Island No. 10, and in the advance on Corinth, Mississippi; in July he assumed command of an infantry division and in September was promoted to major general, U.S. Volunteers; from November 1862 through January 1863, Granger headed the District of Central Kentucky and, thereafter, the Army of Kentucky; in June 1863 he took command of the Reserve Corps, Army of the Cumberland, with which he played a major role in the September 1863 Battle of Chickamauga; there, following the collapse of the Federal army, Granger, on his own initiative, rushed the Reserve Corps to the relief of General George Thomas, helping to save the Army of the Cumberland from possible destruction; Granger then commanded the Fourth Corps, Army of the Cumberland, at Chattanooga and at Knoxville; after a leave of absence, during which he missed the Atlanta Campaign, Granger assumed command of the District of South Alabama; in the closing stages of the war he directed the Thirteenth Corps in the Department of the Gulf, participating in the capture of Forts Gaines and Morgan and, ultimately, Mobile; brevetted through major general, U.S. Army, he continued in the regular army as colonel of the 15th Infantry; plagued by recurring poor health, General Granger died on active duty at Santa Fe, New Mexico Territory, in 1876.

orders would have to stretch to allow him to move down and join the fray. Clearly something decisive was taking place, and all the army should be there to help decide it. So, in the classic move of great generals throughout military history (of which, in all fairness, Granger was not one) the commander of the Reserve Corps marched two of his brigades to the sound of the guns. He could not have arrived at a more opportune moment. Thomas knew just where he was needed and had him rush his men out to the right flank beyond the 21st Ohio. Their arrival prevented a disaster from which few of the units either on Snodgrass Hill or in Kelly Field would have escaped intact.

As welcome as Granger's additional manpower was the large supply of ammunition he brought with him. Without it, the Federals could not have waged the battle they did on Snodgrass Hill and Horseshoe Ridge, hour after hour, all through the afternoon and into the evening. Casualties mounted, with some Union regiments losing half their men. For the Confederates, charging again and again over open ground, the slaughter was at least as bad.

Late that afternoon, a message finally arrived from Rosecrans. He was on his way back to Chattanooga now, and his orders were to retreat. That was no easy task under the constant Confederate pressure on the Snodgrass Hill front. It was about to get harder.

Since the abject failure of the morning and midday assaults on Thomas's Kelly Field perimeter, quiet had prevailed in the blood-soaked woods in front of the Federal battle line. When Longstreet, flushed with his success at the other end of the line, had urged Bragg to renew the assaults by the army's right wing. "There is not a man in the right wing who has any fight in him," replied the disgusted Bragg. By 5:00 P.M., however, the left wing had regrouped and was ready to take up the battle again.

It did so at the worst of all possible times for Thomas. As the Confederates advanced again toward the breastworks before which so many of their comrades had been slaughtered earlier that day, the troops who had been holding those works were just in the process of pulling back into and across Kelly Field. Since the Snodgrass Hill position covered the only line of retreat for all the troops, the Dry Valley Road, the Kelly Field troops had to pull out first. When they were caught in the act, pandemonium resulted. Some units got off in fairly good order. Others went completely to pieces or were all but cut off and had to run a deadly gauntlet of fire before their survivors could escape. Confederates swarmed over the breastworks and into Kelly Field, and a Rebel artillery battery even came

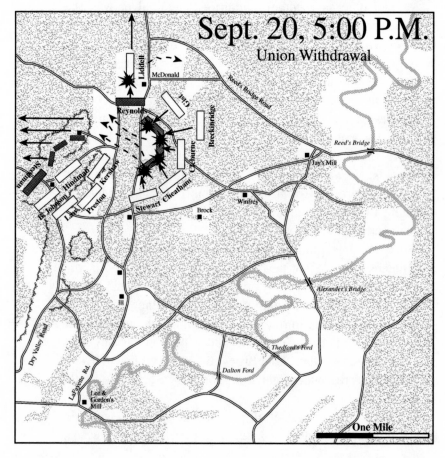

galloping through, swung into line, and started blasting loads of canister into the fleeing Union troops. As Confederates from all sides of the semicircular perimeter met in Kelly Field, they believed they had annihilated a major segment of the Union army, and raised a mighty Rebel yell that could be heard all over the battlefield.

Nevertheless, most of the Federal units had gotten away intact, and some even had a good bit of fight left in them. When Reynolds's Division was ordered to push back a Confederate division that was threatening to sweep down the La Fayette Road and cut off retreat from Kelly Field before most of the units could make their escape, Reynolds confused his orders and thought he was intended to cut a way out for the whole army to follow. Accordingly, he moved up the La Fayette Road, easily swatted the Rebel division out of the way, then proceeded on back to Chattanooga, without further molestation—on a route that was supposedly closed to the Federals.

The rest of the army pulled back through the Snodgrass Field, along Horseshoe Ridge, and down onto the Dry Valley Road. Then, in the gathering twilight, the troops on the open Snodgrass Hill drew back up from the positions they had held all afternoon onto the Horseshoe Ridge. A retreat like this, in the face of an aggressive enemy, over rugged ground, would have been a confused affair even with relatively fresh and well-organized troops. With the hodge-podge of shot-up, played-out units on Horseshoe Ridge, gaping holes in their chains-of-command, it was a very muddled affair indeed. Confused clashes flared up as Confederates, probing gingerly forward through the fast-darkening woods, blundered into the last Union regiments covering the retreat. Not all the regiments on the ridge got the word about the retreat, and that added to the Confederates' bag of prisoners. Among those units that went almost entire into captivity was the 21st Ohio, heroes of one of the war's epic defensive stands on Horseshoe Ridge.

Night finally closed the battle. Those Federals not already

prisoners of war had by now succeeded in disengaging and making good their escape. The next day the Army of the Cumberland began establishing itself in Chattanooga, while Thomas kept his force at Rossville before withdrawing into Chattanooga the day after. Bragg and his men were left to contemplate the battlefield and its harrowing scenes. Some 34,624 men had fallen, 18,454 Confederates and 16,170 Federals, about 28 percent of the men each side had sent into battle. Each army, through loss of equipment, horses, and key personnel, was seriously crippled from undertaking immediate further operations. Bragg realized this quickly. He had ordered a pursuit immediately after the battle, but recognized that his army simply was not fit to carry it out and cancelled the order.

Thus, Chickamauga became another of those Civil War battles in which the defeated army remained intact and little more damaged—materially—than the victor. The key to that result, in this case, had been the failure of all of Bragg's schemes to turn the northern flank of the Army of the Cumberland and cut it off from its base. Such a move, if successful, could have produced truly decisive results. That it did not come to pass was partially due to Rosecrans's and Thomas's alertness in sidling the Army of the Cumberland rapidly northward toward Chattanooga and in keeping the Union northern flank strong enough to resist Bragg's attempts to break it. Partially it was due to the fractious and irresponsible behavior of Bragg's own generals, who contributed enormously to the hollowness of the victory, for which they were quick to blame their commander.

Bragg followed up his victory by besieging Rosecrans in Chattanooga. Though he did not invest the city on the rugged heights of Walden's Ridge to the north, that gap allowed only scant supplies to reach the city, and Rosecrans's men were soon on very short rations indeed. For a time, it looked as if Bragg's Chickamauga victory might not have been so hollow after all. In the end, however, Bragg failed to take Chattanooga or the Army of the Cumberland. Before the struggle for the city was over, he was to test his mettle against the Union's first team, the winning combination of commanders that brought ultimate Northern victory a year and a half later. If Bragg got much the worse of the encounter, he at least had good company.

Union hopes in the region took a dramatic turn for the better in late October, when a new Federal general came to take over affairs on the Chattanooga front. Like Rosecrans, he had been born in Ohio, but he was like him in almost no other way. A quiet man, with an unassuming self-confidence, he had a businesslike determination to get the job done. His name was Ulysses S. Grant.

Note: The Tables of Organization presented in Appendices A and B are taken from *War of the Rebellion: Official Records of the Union and Confederate Armies*, Series I, Volume 30, Part 1, Pages 40–47, and Part 2, Pages 11–20.

APPENDIX A

ORGANIZATION OF FEDERAL FORCES
ARMY OF THE CUMBERLAND
MAJ. GEN. WILLIAM S. ROSECRANS

GENERAL HEADQUARTERS
1ST BATTALION OHIO SHARPSHOOTERS, CAPT. GERSHOM M. BARBER
10TH OHIO INFANTRY, LIEUT. COL. WILLIAM M. WARD
15TH PENNSYLVANIA CAVALRY, COL. WILLIAM J. PALMER

FOURTEENTH ARMY CORPS
MAJ. GEN. GEORGE H. THOMAS

PROVOST GUARD
9TH MICHIGAN INFANTRY, COL. JOHN G. PARKHURST

ESCORT
1ST OHIO CAVALRY, COMPANY L, CAPT. JOHN D. BARKER

FIRST DIVISION
BRIG. GEN. ABSALOM BAIRD

First Brigade
COL. BENJAMIN F. SCRIBNER
38th Indiana, Lieut. Col. Daniel F. Griffin
2d Ohio, Lieut. Col. Obadiah C. Maxwell
33d Ohio, Col. Oscar F. Moore
94th Ohio, Maj. Rue P. Hutchins
10th Wisconsin, Lieut. Col. John H. Ely

Second Brigade
BRIG. GEN. JOHN C. STARKWEATHER
24th Illinois, Col. Geza Mihalotzy
79th Pennsylvania, Col. Henry A. Hambright
1st Wisconsin, Lieut. Col. George B. Bingham
21st Wisconsin, Lieut. Col. Harrison C. Hobart

Third Brigade
BRIG. GEN. JOHN H. KING

15th United States, 1st Battalion, Capt. Albert B. Dod
16th United States, 1st Battalion, Maj. Sidney Coolidge
18th United States, 1st Battalion, Capt. George W. Smith
18th United States, 2d Battalion, Capt. Henry Haymond
19th United States, 1st Battalion, Maj. Samuel K. Dawson

Artillery
Indiana Light, 4th Battery, Lieut. David Flansburg
1st Michigan Light, Battery A, Lieut. George W. Van Pelt
5th United States, Battery H, Lieut. Howard M. Burnham

SECOND DIVISION
MAJ. GEN. JAMES S. NEGLEY

First Brigade
BRIG. GEN. JOHN BEATTY

104th Illinois, Lieut. Col. Douglas Hapeman
42d Indiana, Lieut. Col. William T.B. McIntire
88th Indiana, Col. George Humphrey
15th Kentucky, Col. Marion C. Taylor

Second Brigade
COL. TIMOTHY R. STANLEY

19th Illinois, Lieut. Col. Alexander W. Raffen
11th Michigan, Col. William L. Stoughton
18th Ohio, Lieut. Col. Charles H. Grosvenor

Third Brigade
COL. WILLIAM SIRWELL

37th Indiana, Lieut. Col. William D. Ward
21st Ohio, Lieut. Col. Dwella M. Stoughton
74th Ohio, Capt. Joseph Fisher
78th Pennsylvania, Lieut. Col. Archibald Blakeley

Artillery
Illinois Light, Bridges' Battery, Capt. Lyman Bridges
1st Ohio Light, Battery G, Capt. Alexander Marshall
1st Ohio Light, Battery M, Capt. Frederick Schultz

THIRD DIVISION
BRIG. GEN. JOHN M. BRANNAN

First Brigade
COL. JOHN M. CONNELL
82d Indiana, Col. Morton C. Hunter
17th Ohio, Lieut. Col. Durbin Ward
31st Ohio, Lieut. Col. Frederick W. Lister
38th Ohio, Col. Edward H. Phelps

Second Brigade
COL. JOHN T. CROXTON
10th Indiana, Col. William B. Carroll
74th Indiana, Col. Charles W. Chapman
4th Kentucky, Lieut. Col. P. Burgess Hunt
10th Kentucky, Col. William H. Hays
14th Ohio, Lieut. Col. Henry D. Kingsbury

Third Brigade
COL. FERDINAND VAN DERVEER
87th Indiana, Col. Newell Gleason
2d Minnesota, Col. James George
9th Ohio, Col. Gustave Kammerling
35th Ohio, Lieut. Col. Henry V.N. Boynton

Artillery
1st Michigan Light, Battery D, Josiah W. Church
1st Ohio Light, Battery C, Lieut. Marco B. Gary
4th United States, Battery I, Lieut. Frank G. Smith.

FOURTH DIVISION
MAJ. GEN. JOSEPH J. REYNOLDS

First Brigade
COL. JOHN T. WILDER
92d Illinois, Col. Smith D. Atkins
98th Illinois, Col. John J. Funkhouser
123d Illinois, Col. James Monroe
17th Indiana, Maj. William T. Jones
72nd Indiana, Col. Abram O. Miller

Second Brigade
COL. EDWARD A. KING
68th Indiana, Capt. Harvey J. Espy
75th Indiana, Col. Milton S. Robinson
101st Indiana, Lieut. Col. Thomas Doan
105th Ohio, Maj. George T. Perkins

Third Brigade
BRIG. GEN. JOHN B. TURCHIN
18th Kentucky, Lieut. Col. Hubbard K. Milward
11th Ohio, Col. Philander P. Lane
36th Ohio, Col. William G. Jones
92nd Ohio, Col. Benjamin D. Fearing

Artillery
Indiana Light, 18th Battery, Capt. Eli Lilly
Indiana Light, 19th Battery, Capt. Samuel J. Harris
Indiana Light, 21st Battery, Capt. William W. Andrew

TWENTIETH ARMY CORPS
MAJ. GEN. ALEXANDER MCDOWELL MCCOOK

PROVOST GUARD
81ST INDIANA INFANTRY, COMPANY H, CAPT. WILLIAM J. RICHARDS

ESCORT
2D KENTUCKY CAVALRY, COMPANY I, LIEUT. GEORGE W. L. BATMAN

FIRST DIVISION
BRIG. GEN. JEFFERSON C. DAVIS

First Brigade
COL. SIDNEY POST
59th Illinois, Lieut. Col. Joshua C. Winters
74th Illinois, Col. Jason Marsh
75th Illinois, Col. John E. Bennett
22d Indiana, Col. Michael Gooding
Wisconsin Light Artillery, 5th Battery, Capt. George Q. Gardner

Second Brigade

BRIG. GEN. WILLIAM P. CARLIN

21st Illinois, Col. John W. S. Alexander

38th Illinois, Lieut. Col. Daniel H. Gilmer

81st Indiana, Capt. Nevil B. Boone

101st Ohio, Lieut. Col. John Messer

Minnesota Light Artillery, 2d Battery, Lieut. Albert Woodbury

Third Brigade

COL. HANS C. HEG

25th Illinois, Maj. Samuel D. Wall

35th Illinois, Lieut. Col. William P. Chandler

8th Kansas, Col. John A. Martin

15th Wisconsin, Lieut. Col. Ole C. Johnson

Wisconsin Light Artillery, 8th Battery, Lieut. John D. McLean

SECOND DIVISION

BRIG. GEN. RICHARD W. JOHNSON

First Brigade

BRIG. GEN. AUGUST WILLICH

89th Illinois, Lieut. Col. Duncan J. Hall

32d Indiana, Lieut. Col. Frank Erdelmeyer

39th Indiana, Col. Thomas J. Harrison

15th Ohio, Lieut. Col. Frank Askew

49th Ohio, Maj. Samuel F. Gray

1st Ohio Light Artillery, Battery A, Capt. Wilbur F. Goodspeed

Second Brigade

COL. JOSEPH B. DODGE

79th Illinois, Col. Allen Buckner

29th Indiana, Lieut. Col. David M. Dunn

30th Indiana, Lieut. Col. Orrin D. Hurd

77th Pennsylvania, Col. Thomas E. Rose

Ohio Light Artillery, 20th Battery, Capt. Edward Grosskopff

Third Brigade

COL. PHILEMON P. BALDWIN

6th Indiana, Lieut. Col. Hagerman Tripp

5th Kentucky, Col. William W. Berry

1st Ohio, Lieut. Col Bassett Langdon

93rd Ohio, Col. Hiram Strong

Indiana Light Artillery, 5th Battery, Capt. Peter Simonson

THIRD DIVISION
MAJ. GEN. PHILIP H. SHERIDAN

First Brigade
BRIG. GEN. WILLIAM H. LYTLE

36th Illinois, Col. Silas Miller

88th Illinois, Lieut. Col. Alexander S. Chadbourne

21st Michigan, Col. William B. McCreery

24th Wisconsin, Lieut. Col. Theodore S. West

Indiana Light Artillery, 11th Battery, Capt. Arnold Sutermeister

Second Brigade
COL. BERNARD LAIBOLDT

44th Illinois, Col. Wallace W. Barrett

73d Illinois, Col. James F. Jaquess

2d Missouri, Maj. Arnold Beck

15th Missouri, Col. Joseph Conrad

1st Missouri Light Artillery, Battery G, Lieut. Gustavus Schueler

Third Brigade
COL. LUTHER P. BRADLEY

22d Illinois, Lieut. Col. Francis Swanwick

27th Illinois, Col. Jonathan R. Miles

42d Illinois, Col. Nathan H. Walworth

51st Illinois, Lieut. Col. Samuel B. Raymond

1st Illinois Light Artillery, Battery C, Capt. Mark H. Prescott

TWENTY-FIRST ARMY CORPS
MAJ. GEN. THOMAS L. CRITTENDEN

ESCORT
15TH ILLINOIS CAVALRY, COMPANY K, CAPT. SAMUEL B. SHERER

FIRST DIVISION
BRIG. GEN. THOMAS J. WOOD

First Brigade

COL. GEORGE P. BUELL

100th Illinois, Col. Frederick A. Bartleson

58th Indiana, Lieut. Col. James T. Embree

13th Michigan, Col. Joshua B. Culver

26th Ohio, Lieut. Col. William H. Young

Second Brigade

BRIG. GEN. GEORGE D. WAGNER

15th Indiana, Col. Gustavus A. Wood

40th Indiana, Col. John W. Blake

57th Indiana, Lieut. Col. George W. Lennard

97th Ohio, Lieut. Col. Milton Barnes

Third Brigade

COL. CHARLES G. HARKER

3d Kentucky, Col. Henry C. Dunlap

64th Ohio, Col. Alexander McIlvain

65th Ohio, Lieut. Col. Horatio N. Whitbeck

125th Ohio, Col. Emerson Opdycke

Artillery

Indiana Light, 8th Battery, Capt. George Estep

Indiana Light, 10th Battery, Lieut. William A. Naylor

Ohio Light, 6th Battery, Capt. Cullen Bradley

SECOND DIVISION

MAJ. GEN. JOHN M. PALMER

First Brigade

BRIG. GEN. CHARLES CRUFT

31st Indiana, Col. John T. Smith

1st Kentucky, Lieut. Col. Alva R. Hadlock

2d Kentucky, Col. Thomas D. Sedgewick

90th Ohio, Col. Charles H. Rippey

Second Brigade

BRIG. GEN. WILLIAM B. HAZEN

9th Indiana, Col. Isaac C. B. Suman

6th Kentucky, Col. George T. Shackelford

41st Ohio, Col. Aquila Wiley

124th Ohio, Col. Oliver H. Payne

Third Brigade

COL. WILLIAM GROSE

84th Illinois, Col. Louis H. Waters
36th Indiana, Lieut. Col. Oliver H.P. Carey
23d Kentucky, Lieut. Col. James C. Foy
6th Ohio, Col. Nicholas L. Anderson
24th Ohio, Col. David J. Higgins

ARTILLERY

1st Ohio Light, Battery B, Lieut. Norman A. Baldwin
1st Ohio Light, Battery F, Lieut. Giles J. Cockerill
4th United States, Battery H, Lieut. Harry C. Cushing
4th United States, Battery M, Lieut. Francis L.D. Russell

Unattached

110th Illinois (battalion), Capt. E. Hibbard Topping

THIRD DIVISION

BRIG. GEN. HORATIO P. VAN CLEVE

First Brigade

BRIG. GEN. SAMUEL BEATTY

79th Indiana, Col. Frederick Knefler
9th Kentucky, Col. George H. Cram
17th Kentucky, Col. Alexander M. Stout
19th Ohio, Lieut. Col. Henry D. Stratton

Second Brigade

COL. GEORGE F. DICK

44th Indiana, Lieut. Col. Simeon C. Aldrich
86th Indiana, Maj. Jacob C. Dick
13th Ohio, Lieut. Col. Elhannon M. Mast
59th Ohio, Lieut. Col. Granville A. Frambes

Third Brigade

COL. SIDNEY M. BARNES

35th Indiana, Maj. John P. Dufficy
8th Kentucky, Lieut. Col. James D. Mayhew
21st Kentucky, Col. S. Woodson Price
51st Ohio, Col. Richard W. McClain
99th Ohio, Col. Peter T. Swaine

Artillery

Indiana Light, 7th Battery, Capt. George R. Swallow

Pennsylvania Light, 26th Battery, Capt. Alanson J. Stevens

Wisconsin Light, 3d Battery, Lieut. Cortland Livingston

RESERVE CORPS
MAJ. GEN. GORDON GRANGER

FIRST DIVISION
BRIG. GEN. JAMES B. STEEDMAN

First Brigade

Brig. Gen. Walter C. Whitaker

96th Illinois, Col. Thomas E. Champion

115th Illinois, Col. Jesse H. Moore

84th Indiana, Col. Nelson Trusler

22d Michigan, Col. Heber Le Favour

40th Ohio, Lieut. Col. William Jones

89th Ohio, Col. Caleb H. Carlton

Ohio Light Artillery, 18th Battery, Capt. Charles C. Aleshire

Second Brigade

COL. JOHN G. MITCHELL

78th Illinois, Lieut. Col. Carter Van Vleck

98th Ohio, Capt. Moses J. Urquhart

113th Ohio, Lieut. Col. Darius B. Warner

121st Ohio, Lieut. Col. Henry B. Banning

1st Illinois Light Artillery, Battery M, Lieut. Thomas Burton

SECOND DIVISION

Second Brigade

COL. DANIEL McCOOK

85th Illinois, Col. Caleb J. Dilworth

86th Illinois, Lieut. Col. David W. Magee

125th Illinois, Col. Oscar F. Harmon

52nd Ohio, Maj. James T. Holmes

69th Ohio, Lieut. Col. Joseph H. Brigham

2d Illinois Light Artillery, Battery I, Capt. Charles M. Barnett

CAVALRY CORPS
BRIG. GEN. ROBERT B. MITCHELL

FIRST DIVISION
COL. EDWARD M. MCCOOK

First Brigade
COL. ARCHIBALD P. CAMPBELL
2d Michigan, Maj. Leonidas S. Scranton
9th Pennsylvania, Lieut. Col. Roswell M. Russell
1st Tennessee, Lieut. Col. James P. Brownlow

Second Brigade
COL. DANIEL M. RAY
2d Indiana, Maj. Joseph B. Presdee
4th Indiana, Lieut. Col. John T. Deweese
2d Tennessee, Lieut. Col. William R. Cook
1st Wisconsin, Col. Oscar H. LaGrange
1st Ohio Light Artillery, Battery D (section),
Lieut. Nathaniel M. Newell

Third Brigade
COL. LOUIS D. WATKINS
4th Kentucky, Col. Wickliffe Cooper
5th Kentucky, Lieut. Col. William T. Hoblitzell
6th Kentucky, Maj. Louis A. Gratz

SECOND DIVISION
BRIG. GEN. GEORGE CROOK

First Brigade
COL. ROBERT H. G. MINTY
3d Indiana (battalion), Lieut. Col. Robert Klein
4th Michigan, Maj. Horace Gray
7th Pennsylvania, Lieut. Col. James J. Seibert
4th United States, Capt. James B. McIntyre

Second Brigade
COL. ELI LONG
2d Kentucky, Col. Thomas P. Nicholas
1st Ohio, Lieut. Col. Valentine Cupp
3d Ohio, Lieut. Col. Charles B. Seidel
4th Ohio, Lieut. Col. Oliver P. Robie

Artillery
Chicago Board of Trade Battery, Capt. James H. Stokes

APPENDIX B

ORGANIZATION OF CONFEDERATE FORCES
ARMY OF TENNESSEE
GEN. BRAXTON BRAGG

ESCORT
DREUX'S COMPANY LOUISIANA CAVALRY, LIEUT. O. DE BUIS
HOLLOWAY'S COMPANY ALABAMA CAVALRY, CAPT. E. M. HOLLOWAY

RIGHT WING
LIEUT. GEN. LEONIDAS POLK

ESCORT
GREENLEAF'S COMPANY LOUISIANA CAVALRY, CAPT. LEEDS GREENLEAF

CHEATHAM'S DIVISION
MAJ. GEN. BENJAMIN F. CHEATHAM

ESCORT
COMPANY G, 2D GEORGIA CAVALRY, CAPT. THOMAS M. MERRITT

Jackson's Brigade
BRIG. GEN. JOHN K. JACKSON
1st Georgia, 2d Battalion, Maj. James Clarke Gordon
5th Georgia, Col. Charles P. Daniel
2d Georgia Battalion Sharpshooters, Maj. Richard H. Whiteley
5th Mississippi, Lieut. Col. W.L. Sykes
8th Mississippi, Col. John C. Wilkinson

Smith's Brigade
BRIG. GEN. PRESTON SMITH
11th Tennessee, Col. George W. Gordon
12th and 47th Tennessee, Col. William M. Watkins
13th and 154th Tennessee, Col. A.J. Vaughan, Jr.
29th Tennessee, Col. Horace Rice
Dawson's (battalion) Sharpshooters, Maj. J.W. Dawson

Maney's Brigade
BRIG. GEN. GEORGE MANEY
1st and 27th Tennessee, Col. Hume R. Field
4th Tennessee, Col. James A. McMurry
6th and 9th Tennessee, Col. George C. Porter
24th Tennessee Battalion Sharpshooters, Maj. Frank Maney

Wright's Brigade
BRIG. GEN. MARCUS J. WRIGHT
8th Tennessee, Col. John H. Anderson
16th Tennessee, Col. D.M. Donnell
28th Tennessee, Col. Sidney S. Stanton
38th Tennessee and Murray's Tennessee Battalion, Col. John C. Carter
51st and 52d Tennessee, Lieut. Col. John G. Hall

Strahl's Brigade
BRIG. GEN. OTHO F. STRAHL
4th and 5th Tennessee, Col. Jonathan J. Lamb
19th Tennessee, Col. Francis M. Walker
24th Tennessee, Col. John A. Wilson
31st Tennessee, Col. Egbert E. Tansil
33d Tennessee, Col. Warner P. Jones

Artillery
MAJ. MELANCTHON SMITH
Carnes' Tennessee Battery, Capt. William W. Carnes
Scogin's Georgia Battery, Capt. John Scogin
Scott's Tennessee Battery, Lieut. John H. Marsh
Smith's Mississippi Battery, Lieut. William B. Turner
Stanford's Mississippi Battery, Capt. Thomas J. Stanford

HILL'S CORPS
LIEUT. GEN. DANIEL H. HILL

CLEBURNE'S DIVISION
MAJ. GEN. PATRICK R. CLEBURNE

ESCORT
SANDERS' COMPANY TENNESSEE CAVALRY, CAPT. C. F. SANDERS

Wood's Brigade
BRIG. GEN. S.A.M. WOOD

16th Alabama, Maj. John H. McGaughy
33d Alabama, Col. Samuel Ashford
45th Alabama, Col. E.B. Breedlove
18th Alabama Battalion, Maj. John H. Gibson
32d and 45th Mississippi, Col. M.P. Lowrey
15th Mississippi Battalion Sharpshooters, Maj. A.T. Hawkins

Polk's Brigade
BRIG. GEN. LUCIUS E. POLK

1st Arkansas, Col. John W. Colquitt
3d and 5th Confederate, Col. J.A. Smith
2d Tennessee, Col. William D. Robison
35th Tennessee, Col. Benjamin J. Hill
48th Tennessee, Col. George H. Nixon

Deshler's Brigade
Brig. Gen. James Deshler
9th and 24th Arkansas, Lieut. Col. A.S. Hutchison
6th and 10th Texas Infantry and 15th Texas Cavalry (dismounted),
Col. Roger Q. Mills
17th, 18th, 24th, and 25th Texas Cavalry (dismounted), Col. F.C. Wilkes

Artillery
MAJ. T.R. HOTCHKISS

Calvert's Arkansas Battery, Lieut. Thomas J. Key
Douglas' Texas Battery, Capt. James P. Douglas
Semple's Alabama Battery, Capt. Henry C. Semple

BRECKINRIDGE'S DIVISION
MAJ. GEN. JOHN C. BRECKINRIDGE

ESCORT
FOULES' COMPANY MISSISSIPPI CAVALRY, CAPT. H. L. FOULES

Helm's Brigade
Brig. Gen. Benjamin H. Helm
41st Alabama, Col. Martin L. Stansel

2d Kentucky, Lieut. Col. James W. Hewitt
4th Kentucky, Col. Joseph P. Nuckols
6th Kentucky, Col. Joseph H. Lewis
9th Kentucky, Col. John W. Caldwell

Adams' Brigade
BRIG. GEN. DANIEL W. ADAMS
32d Alabama, Maj. John C. Kimbell
13th and 20th Louisiana, Col. Randall L. Gibson
16th and 25th Louisiana, Col. Daniel Gober
19th Louisiana, Lieut. Col. Richard W. Turner
14th Louisiana Battalion, Maj. J. E. Austin

Stovall's Brigade
BRIG. GEN. MARCELLUS A. STOVALL
1st and 3d Florida, Col. William S. Dilworth
4th Florida, Col. W. L. L. Bowen
47th Georgia, Capt. William S. Phillips
60th North Carolina, Lieut. Col. James M. Ray

Artillery
MAJ. RICE E. GRAVES
Cobb's Kentucky Battery, Capt. Robert Cobb
Graves' Kentucky Battery, Lieut. S.M. Spencer
Mebane's Tennessee Battery, Capt. John W. Mebane
Slocomb's Louisiana Battery, Capt. C.H. Slocomb

RESERVE CORPS
MAJ. GEN. WILLIAM H.T. WALKER

WALKER'S DIVISION
BRIG. GEN. STATES RIGHTS GIST

Gist's Brigade
COL. PEYTON H. COLQUITT
46th Georgia, Maj. A.M. Speer
8th Georgia Battalion, Lieut. Col. Leroy Napier
16th South Carolina, Col. James McCullough
24th South Carolina, Col. Clement H. Stevens

Ector's Brigade
BRIG. GEN. MATTHEW D. ECTOR
Stone's Alabama Battalion Sharpshooters, Maj. T.O. Stone
Pound's Mississippi Battalion Sharpshooters, Capt. M. Pound
29th North Carolina, Col. William B. Creasman
9th Texas, Col. William H. Young
10th Texas Cavalry (dismounted), Lieut. Col. C.R. Earp
14th Texas Cavalry (dismounted), Col. J.L. Camp
32d Texas Cavalry (dismounted), Col. Julius A. Andrews

Wilson's Brigade
COL. CLAUDIUS C. WILSON
25th Georgia, Lieut. Col. A.J. Williams
29th Georgia, Lieut. George R. McRae
30th Georgia, Lieut. Col. James S. Boynton
1st Georgia Battalion Sharpshooters, Maj. Arthur Shaaff
4th Louisiana Battalion, Lieut. Col. John McEnery

Artillery
Ferguson's South Carolina Battery, Lieut. R.T. Beauregard
Howell's Georgia Battery, Capt. Evan P. Howell

LIDDELL'S DIVISION
BRIG. GEN. ST. JOHN R. LIDDELL

Liddell's Brigade
COL. DANIEL C. GOVAN
2d and 15th Arkansas, Lieut. Col. Reuben F. Harvey
5th and 13th Arkansas, Col. L. Featherston
6th and 7th Arkansas, Col. D.A. Gillespie
8th Arkansas, Lieut. Col. George F. Baucum
1st Louisiana, Maj. A. Watkins

Walthall's Brigade
BRIG. GEN. EDWARD C. WALTHALL
24th Mississippi, Lieut. Col. R.P. McKelvaine
27th Mississippi, Col. James A. Campbell
29th Mississippi, Col. William F. Brantly
30th Mississippi, Col. Junius I. Scales
34th Mississippi, Maj. William G. Pegram

Artillery
CAPT. CHARLES SWETT
Fowler's Alabama Battery, Capt. William H. Fowler
Warren (Mississippi) Light Artillery (battery), Lieut. H. Shannon

LEFT WING
LIEUT. GEN. JAMES LONGSTREET

HINDMAN'S DIVISION
MAJ. GEN. THOMAS C. HINDMAN

ESCORT
LENOIR'S COMPANY ALABAMA CAVALRY, CAPT. T. M. LENOIR

Anderson's Brigade
BRIG. GEN. PATTON ANDERSON
7th Mississippi, Col. W.H. Bishop
9th Mississippi, Maj. T.H. Lynam
10th Mississippi, Lieut. Col. James Barr
41th Mississippi, Col. W.F. Tucker
44th Mississippi, Col. J.H. Sharp
9th Mississippi Battalion Sharpshooters, Maj. W. C. Richards
Garrity's Alabama Battery, Capt. James Garrity

Deas' Brigade
BRIG. GEN. ZACHARIAH C. DEAS
19th Alabama, Col. Samuel K. McSpadden
22d Alabama, Lieut. Col. John Weeden
25th Alabama, Col. George D. Johnston
39th Alabama, Col. Whitfield Clark
50th Alabama, Col. J.G. Coltart
17th Alabama Battalion Sharpshooters, Capt. James F. Nabers
Dent's Alabama Battery, Capt. S.H. Dent

Manigault's Brigade
BRIG. GEN. ARTHUR M. MANIGAULT
24th Alabama, Col. N.N. Davis
28th Alabama, Col. John C. Reid
34th Alabama, Maj. John N. Slaughter
10th and 19th South Carolina, Col. James F. Pressley
Waters' Alabama Battery, Lieut. Charles W. Watkins

BUCKNER'S CORPS
MAJ. GEN. SIMON B. BUCKNER

ESCORT
CLARK'S COMPANY TENNESSEE CAVALRY, CAPT. J.W. CLARK

STEWART'S DIVISION
MAJ. GEN. ALEXANDER P. STEWART

Bate's Brigade
BRIG. GEN. WILLIAM B. BATE
58th Alabama, Col. Bushrod Jones
37th Georgia, Col. A.F. Rudler
4th Georgia Battalion Sharpshooters, Maj. T.D. Caswell
15th and 37th Tennessee, Col. R.C. Tyler
20th Tennessee, Col. Thomas B. Smith

Brown's Brigade
BRIG. GEN. JOHN C. BROWN
18th Tennessee, Col. Joseph B. Palmer
26th Tennessee, Col. John M. Lillard
32d Tennessee, Col. Edmund C. Cook
45th Tennessee, Col. Anderson Searcy
23d Tennessee Battalion, Maj. Tazewell W. Newman

Clayton's Brigade
Brig. Gen. Henry D. Clayton
18th Alabama, Col. J.T. Holtzclaw
36th Alabama, Col. Lewis T. Woodruff
38th Alabama, Lieut. Col. A.R. Lankford

Artillery
MAJ. WESLEY ELDRIGE
1st Arkansas Battery, Capt. John T. Humphreys
T. H. Dawson's Gerogia Battery, Lieut. R.W. Anderson
Eufaula (Alabama) Artillery (battery), Capt. McDonald Oliver
Company E, 9th Georgia Artillery Battalion, Lieut. William S. Everett

PRESTON'S DIVISION
BRIG. GEN. WILLIAM PRESTON

Gracie's Brigade
BRIG. GEN. ARCHIBALD GRACIE, JR.
43d Alabama, Col. Young M. Moody
1st Alabama Battalion (Hilliard's Legion), Lieut. Col. John H. Holt
2nd Alabama Battalion (Hilliard's Legion), Lieut. Col. Bolling Hall, Jr.
3rd Alabama Battalion (Hilliard's Legion),
Lieut. Col. John W.A. Sanford
4th Alabama Battalion (Hilliard's Legion), Maj. John D. McLennan
63d Tennessee, Lieut. Col. Abraham Fulkerson

Trigg's Brigade
COL. ROBERT C. TRIGG
1st Florida Cavalry (dismounted), Col. G. Troup Maxwell
6th Florida, Col. J.J. Finley
7th Florida, Col. Robert Bullock
54th Virginia, Lieut. Col. John J. Wade

Third Brigade
COL. JOHN H. KELLY
65th Georgia, Col. R.H. Moore
5th Kentucky, Col. Hiram Hawkins
58th North Carolina, Col. John B. Palmer
63d Virginia, Maj. James M. French
Artillery
Maj. A. Leyden
Jeffress' Virginia Battery, Capt. William C. Jeffress
Peeples' Georgia Battery, Capt. Tyler M. Peeples
Wolihin's Georgia Battery, Capt. Andrew M. Wolihin

LONGSTREET'S CORPS
MAJ. GEN. JOHN B. HOOD

MCLAW'S DIVISION
BRIG. GEN. JOSEPH B. KERSHAW

Kershaw's Brigade
BRIG. GEN. JOSEPH B. KERSHAW
2d South Carolina, Lieut. Col. Franklin Gaillard
3d South Carolina, Col. James D. Nance
7th South Carolina, Lieut. Col. Elbert Bland
8th South Carolina, Col. John W. Henagan
15th South Carolina, Col. Joseph F. Gist
3d South Carolina Battalion, Capt. Joshua M. Townsend

Humphreys' Brigade
BRIG. GEN. BENJAMIN G. HUMPHREYS
13th Mississippi, Lieut. Col. Kennon McElroy
17th Mississippi, Lieut. Col. John C. Fiser
18th Mississippi, Capt. W. F. Hubbard
21st Mississippi, Lieut. Col. D. N. Moody

HOOD'S DIVISION
BRIG. GEN. E. McIVER LAW

Law's Brigade
COL. JAMES L. SHEFFIELD
4th Alabama, Col. Pinckney D. Bowles
15th Alabama, Col. W.C. Oates
44th Alabama, Col. William F. Perry
47th Alabama, Maj. James M. Campbell
48th Alabama, Lieut. Col. William M. Hardwick

Robertson's Brigade
BRIG. GEN. JEROME B. ROBERTSON
3d Arkansas, Col. Van H. Manning
1st Texas, Capt. R.J. Harding
4th Texas, Lieut. Col. John P. Bane
5th Texas, Maj. J.C. Rogers

Anderson's Brigade
BRIG. GEN. GEORGE T. ANDERSON
7th Georgia, —
8th Georgia, —
9th Georgia, —
11th Georgia, —
59th Georgia, —

Benning's Brigade

BRIG. GEN. HENRY L. BENNING

2d Georgia, Lieut. Col. William S. Shepherd

15th Georgia, Col. Dudley M. Du Bose

17th Georgia, Lieut. Col. Charles W. Matthews

20th Georgia, Col. J.D. Waddell

RESERVE ARTILLERY

MAJ. FELIX H. ROBERTSON

Barret's Missouri Battery, Capt. Overton W. Barret

Le Gardeur's Louisiana Battery, Capt. G. Le Gardeur, Jr.

Havis' Georgia Battery, Capt. M.W. Havis

Lumsden's Alabama Battery, Capt. Charles L. Lumsden

Massenburg's Georgia Battery, Capt. T.L. Massenburg

CAVALRY

MAJ. GEN. JOSEPH WHEELER

WHARTON'S DIVISION

BRIG. GEN. JOHN A. WHARTON

First Brigade

COL. C. C. CREWS

Malone's Alabama Regiment, Col. J.C. Malone, Jr.

2d Georgia, Lieut. Col. F.M. Ison

3d Georgia, Col. R. Thompson

4th Georgia, Col. Isaac W. Avery

Second Brigade

COL. THOMAS HARRISON

3d Confederate, Col. W.N. Estes

3d Kentucky, Lieut. Col.J.W. Griffin

4th Tennessee, Lieut. Col. Paul F. Anderson

8th Texas, Lieut. Col. Gustave Cook

11th Texas, Col. G.R. Reeves

White's Tennessee Battery, Capt. B.F. White, Jr.

MARTIN'S DIVISION
BRIG. GEN. WILLIAM T. MARTIN

First Brigade
COL. JOHN T. MORGAN
1st Alabama, Lieut. Col. D.T. Blakey
3d Alabama, Lieut. Col. T.H. Mauldin
51st Alabama, Lieut. Col. M.L. Kirkpatrick
8th Confederate, Lieut. Col. John S. Prather

Second Brigade
COL. A.A. RUSSELL
4th Alabama, Lieut. Col. J.M. Hambrick
1st Confederate, Capt. C.H. Conner
J. H. Wiggins' Arkansas Battery, Lieut. J.P. Bryant

FORREST'S CORPS
BRIG. GEN. NATHAN B. FORREST

ESCORT
JACKSON'S COMPANY TENNESSEE CAVALRY, CAPT. J. C. JACKSON

ARMSTRONG'S DIVISION
BRIG. GEN. FRANK C. ARMSTRONG

Armstrong's Brigade
COL. JAMES T. WHEELER
3d Arkansas, Col. A.W. Hobson
2d Kentucky, Lieut. Col. Thomas G. Woodward
6th Tennessee, Lieut. Col. James H. Lewis
18th Tennessee Battalion, Maj. Charles McDonald

Forrest's Brigade
COL. GEORGE G. DIBRELL
4th Tennessee, Col. William S. McLemore
8th Tennessee, Capt. Hamilton McGinnis
9th Tennessee, Col. Jacob B. Biffle
10th Tennessee, Col. Nicholas Nickleby Cox
11th Tennessee, Col. Daniel Wilson Holman
Shaw's Battalion, O.P. Hamilton's Battalion, and R.D. Allison's

Squadron (consolidated), Maj. Joseph Shaw
Huggins' Tennessee Battery, Capt. A.L. Huggins
Morton's Tennessee Battery, Capt. John W. Morton, Jr.

PEGRAM'S DIVISION
BRIG. GEN. JOHN PEGRAM

Davidson's Brigade
BRIG. GEN. H. B. DAVIDSON
1st Georgia, Col. J.J. Morrison
6th Georgia, Col John R. Hart
6th North Carolina, Col. George N. Folk
Rucker's (1st Tennessee) Legion, Col. E. W. Rucker
Huwald's Tennessee Battery, Capt. Gustave A. Huwald

Scott's Brigade
COL JOHN S. SCOTT
10th Confederate, Col C.T. Goode
Detachment of John H. Morgan's command, Lieut. Col. R.M. Martin
1st Louisiana, Lieut. Col. James O. Nixon
2d Tennessee, Col. H.M. Ashby
5th Tennessee, Col. George W. McKenzie
N.T.N. Robinson's Louisiana Battery (one section),
Lieut. Winslow Robinson

FURTHER READING

Bowers, John. *Chickamauga and Chattanooga: The Battle That Doomed the Confederacy.* New York: HarperCollins, 1994.

Catton, Bruce. *Never Call Retreat.* Garden City, N.Y.: Doubleday, 1965.

Cist, Henry M. *The Army of the Cumberland.* New York: Charles Scribner's Sons, 1882.

Cleaves, Freeman. *Rock of Chickamauga: The Life of General George H. Thomas.* Norman: University of Oklahoma Press, 1948.

Connelly, Thomas Lawrence. *Autumn of Glory: The Army of Tennessee, 1862-1865.* Baton Rouge and London: Louisiana State University Press, 1971.

Connelly, Thomas Lawrence, and Archer Jones. *The Politics of Command: Factions and Ideas in Confederate Strategy.* Baton Rouge and London: Louisiana State University Press, 1982.

Cozzens, Peter. *This Terrible Sound: The Battle of Chickamauga.* Urbana and Chicago: University of Illinois Press, 1992.

Daniels, Larry J. *Cannoneers in Gray: The Field Artillery of the Army of Tennessee, 1861-1865.* Tuscaloosa and London: University of Alabama Press, 1984.

Davis, William C. *Breckinridge: Statesman, Soldier, Symbol.* Baton Rouge and London: Louisiana State University Press, 1974.

Eckenrode, H. J., and Bryan Conrad. *James Longstreet: Lee's War Horse.* Reprint. Chapel Hill and London: University of North Carolina Press, 1986.

Foote, Shelby. *The Civil War: A Narrative.* Reprint. 3 vols. New York: Vintage Books, 1986.

Gracie, Archibald. *The Truth About Chickamauga.* Boston and New York: Houghton Mifflin, 1911.

Halleck, Judith Lee. *Braxton Bragg and Confederate Defeat.* Vol. 2. Tuscaloosa and London: The University of Alabama Press, 1991.

Hattaway, Herman, and Archer Jones. *How the North Won: A Military History of the Civil War.* Urbana and Chicago: University of Illinois Press, 1983.

Horn, Stanley F. *The Army of Tennessee: A Military History.* Indianapolis and New York: Bobbs-Merrill, 1941.

Hughes, Nathaniel Cheairs. *General William J. Hardee: Old Reliable.* Baton Rouge and London: Louisiana State University Press, 1965.

Johnson, Robert Underwood, and Clarence Clough Buel, eds. *Battles and Leaders of the Civil War.* Reprint. 4 vols. New York: Thomas Yoseloff, Inc., 1956.

Lamers, William. *The Edge of Glory: A Biogrpahy of General William S. Rosecrans, U.S.A.* New York: Harcourt, Brace and World, 1961.

Longstreet, James. *From Manassas to Appomattox: Memoirs of the Civil War in America.* Edited by James I. Robertson, Jr. New ed. Bloomington: Indiana University Press, 1960.

Losson, Christopher. *Tennessee's Forgotten Warriors: Frank Cheatham and His Confederate Division.* Knoxville: University of Tennessee Press, 1989.

McGee, Benjamin. *History of the Seventy-second Indiana Volunteer Infantry.* Lafayette, Ind.: S. Vatter and Company, 1882.

McKinney, Francis. *Education in Violence: The Life of George H. Thomas and the History of the Army of the Cumberland.* Detroit: Wayne State University Press, 1961.

McMurry, Richard M. *John Bell Hood and the War for Southern Independence.* Lexington: University Press of Kentucky, 1982.

Parks, Joseph H. *General Leonidas Polk, C.S.A.: The Fighting Bishop.* Baton Rouge and London: Louisiana State University Press, 1962.

Piston, William Garrett. *Lee's Tarnished Lieutenant: James Longstreet and His Place in Southern History.* Athens and London: University of Georgia Press, 1987.

Polley, Joseph Benjamin. *Hood's Texas Brigade, Its Marches, Its Battles, Its Achievements.* New York and Washington: The Neale Publishing Company, 1910.

Seitz, Don C. *Braxton Bragg: General of the Confederacy.* Columbia, S.C.: The State Company, 1924.

Simpson, Harold B. *Gaines' Mill to Appomattox: Waco & McLennan County in Hood's Texas Brigade.* Waco, Tx.: Texian Press, 1988.

_____. *Hood's Texas Brigade: Lee's Grenadier Guard.* Waco, Tx.: Texian Press, 1970.

Sorrel, G. Moxley. *Recollections of a Confederate Staff Officer.* Reprint. Dayton, Ohio: Morningside Bookshop, 1978.

Tucker, Glenn. *Chickamauga: Bloody Battle in the West.* Indianapolis and New York: Bobbs-Merrill, 1961.

Turchin, John B. *Chickamauga.* Chicago: Fergus, 1888.

Wert, Jeffery D. *General James Longstreet: The Confederacy's Most Controversial Soldier—A Biography.* New York: Simon & Schuster, 1993.

Williams, Samuel. *General John T. Wilder, Commander of the Lightning Brigade.* Bloomington: Indiana University Press, 1936.

Wills, Brian Steel. *A Battle From the Start: The Life of Nathan Bedford Forrest.* New York: HarperCollins, 1992.

Woodworth, Steven E. *Chickamauga: A Battlefield Guide.* Lincoln: University of Nebraska Press, 1997.

_____. *The Chickamauga and Chattanooga Campaign.* Lincoln: University of Nebraska Press, 1997.

_____. *Jefferson Davis and His Generals: The Failure of Confederate Command in the West.* Lawrence: University Press of Kansas, 1990.

PHOTO CREDITS

We acknowledge the cooperation of The Library of Congress, Washington, D.C. for the photographs of Braxton Bragg, Patrick R. Cleburne, James Longstreet, and George H. Thomas.

We acknowledge the cooperation of the U.S. Army Military History Institute at Carlisle Barracks, Pennsylvania for the photographs of John C. Breckinridge, Thomas Leonidas Crittenden, Jefferson C. Davis, Nathan Bedford Forrest, Gordon Granger, William B. Hazen, Daniel H. Hill, John Bell Hood, Bushrod R. Johnson, Joseph Brevard Kershaw, Alexander McDowell McCook, Leonidas Polk, William Starke Rosecrans, Philip Henry Sheridan, Alexander P. Stewart, John Thomas Wilder, and Thomas J. Wood.

Once again we are grateful to Mr. Jim Enos for his expert assistance.

The cover photograph of Chickamauga Creek was furnished by the author, Steven E. Woodworth.

INDEX

Other titles in the Civil War Campaigns and Commanders Series include...

Battle in the Wilderness: Grant Meets Lee by Grady McWhiney ❖ Death in September: The Antietam Campaign by Perry D. Jamieson ❖ Texans in the Confederate Cavalry by Anne J. Bailey ❖ Sam Bell Maxey and the Confederate Indians by John C. Waugh ❖ The Saltville Massacre by Thomas D. Mays ❖ General James Longstreet in the West: A Monumental Failure by Judith Lee Hallock ❖ The Battle of the Crater by Jeff Kinard ❖ Cottonclads! The Battle of Galveston and the Defense of the Texas Coast by Donald S. Frazier ❖ A Deep, Steady Thunder: The Battle of Chickamauga by Steven E. Woodworth ❖ The Texas Overland Expedition by Richard Lowe ❖ Raphael Semmes and the Alabama by Spencer C. Tucker ❖ War in the West: Pea Ridge and Prairie Grove by William L. Shea ❖ Iron and Heavy Guns: Duel Between the Monitor and Merrimac by Gene A. Smith ❖

The Emergence of Total War by Daniel E. Sutherland ❖ John Bell Hood and the Struggle for Atlanta by David Coffey ❖ The Most Promising Young Man of the South: James Johnston Pettigrew and His Men at Gettysburg by Clyde N. Wilson ❖ Vicksburg: Fall of the Confederate Gibraltar by Terrence J. Winschel ❖ This Grand Spectacle: The Battle of Chattanooga by Steven E. Woodworth ❖ Rutherford B. Hayes: "One of the Good Colonels" by Ari Hoogenboom ❖ Jefferson Davis's Greatest General: Albert Sidney Johnston by Charles P. Roland ❖ Unconditional Surrender: The Capture of Forts Henry and Donelson by Spencer C. Tucker ❖ Last Stand at Mobile by John C. Waugh ❖ George Gordon Meade and the War in the East by Ethan S. Rafuse ❖ Winfield Scott Hancock: Gettysburg Hero by Perry D. Jamieson ❖ The Last Stronghold: The Campaign for Fort Fisher by Richard B. McCaslin ❖ Sherman's March to the Sea by John Marszalek ❖ Campaign for Corinth: Blood in Mississippi by Steven Nathaniel Dossman

These books available at booksellers or through Texas A&M University Press Consortium at 1-800-826-8911 or on-line at www.tamu.edu/upress

CPSIA information can be obtained at www.ICGtesting.com
Printed in the USA
LVOW040147031011

248773LV00003B/4/A